HANDBOOK OF TOURISM ETHICS

HANDBOOK OF
TOURISM ETHICS

Edited by
Shambhu Dayal

AKANSHA PUBLISHING HOUSE
NEW DELHI - 110 059 (INDIA)

AKANSHA PUBLISHING HOUSE
4649/21-B, Ansari Road
Daryaganj, New Delhi - 110 002
Phones: 23263193, 9811582579
E-mail: ektabooks@yahoo.com

Handbook of Tourism Ethics

First Published, 2006

ISBN 81-8370-069-1

PRINTED IN INDIA

Published by M.P. Misra for Akansha Publishing House, New Delhi
and Printed at Aryan Enterprises, Delhi

Contents

Preface

> Our most valuable possessions are those which can be shared without lessening—those which, when shared, multiply. Our least valuable possessions, on the other hand, are those which, when divided, are diminished.
>
> —*William H. Danforth*

Why the need of 'code of ethics' or 'code of conduct' for tourism and hospitality industry? The answer of the question lies in the impact of tourism on environment, economy, culture and society of tourist receiving (i.e. the destination) country or locale.

Here in this book we have reproduced some such select codes with universal or general appeal and acceptability.

This book encompasses vital information on various aspects of tourism ethics, including Introduction; WTO Recommendations to Government for Supporting and/or Establishing National Certification Systems for Sustainable Tourism; Indian Tourism Act and Associated Policy Frameworks; Regulation & Act of Hotel Classification Standards and Hotel Incentives; Global Codes of Ethics for Tourism; Tourism Codes of Conduct and Codes of Ethics; Global Tourism, Tourist Traffic and Tourist Boards Act; Select Visa Rules, Global Holidays Act & Tourism Law contacts. An exhaustive bibliography and glossary of relvant terms are added features of this book. Hopefully, this will serve the purpose of trainers, trainers and professionals in the field.

The entire information is gathered from various authoritative secondary sources, e.g., books, abstracts, catalogues, official documents, and monographs etc. The leading experts and professional's views and experiences are heavily drawn upon for the information. We owe a deep sense of gratitude to them all.

We are thankful to our friends, colleagues and well wishers for extending ready help, assistance and also enthusing our present efforts. Finally, we are thankful to our publishers for bringing out this book superbly within stimulated time period.

Constructive criticism and suggestions are welcome from all quarters for enhancing the quality and utility of this work.

—*Editor*

1

Introduction

Why the need of 'code of ethics' or 'code of conduct' for tourism and hospitality industry? The answer of the question lies in the impact of tourism on environment, economy, culture and society of tourist receiving (i.e. the destination) country or locale.

For example, Tourism in the small islands context involves people who come from other countries for the pleasure of visiting the island environment. Since tourists spend money on travel, hotels, food, entertainment and recreation, they can be an important source of income and thus of economic development for islands with few other possible sources of revenue.

The tourists who come to the islands have been attracted by their image of the island environment: sun and sea, white sandy beaches and waving palm trees, lush vegetation and friendly natives. Or in case of a hilly area, the mountain peaks, forests, valleys, glaciers etc. The reality is never quite the same as the tourist image, but while it can be different, it should not disappoint them or tourism will ultimately fail. People do not come several thousand kilometres to see the same dirt, pollution, industry and degraded environments that they have at home.

Tourism thus depends on the quality of the environment

for its success, and good tourist development requires the protection and even the improvement of the environment. The most important tourism resources are the natural beauty of the island, their distinctive or exotic character, their recreation possibilities, and the cultural interest of the people. The hotels, resorts, transportation networks, recreation facilities and other tourism infrastructure can complement but never completely replace the dependence on environmental resources. The basic problem with tourism development is that tourism facilities and the tourists themselves have impacts on the environment. If care is not taken, the tourism development itself can gradually destroy the environmental resources on which it depends. This problem can be particularly serious on tropical islands where the environment is fragile and easily degraded, and where the small scale of the island means that even moderate tourism development can have a proportionately large impact.

Economic and Social Impacts

The economic and social impacts of tourism are a big subject which can only be examined in detail for any large tourism development project.

Economically, tourism can create jobs for local people and bring money into the country. However many tourists like their comforts from home, and it is often necessary to import a large part of their requirements, so that much of the money may leave the country again to pay for these imports. If the resorts and hotels have been financed by overseas investors, they will also want to export their profits. The developers may want the government to improve the airport, roads and other infrastructure, and possibly to provide tax breaks and other financial advantages, which cost the country money. The remaining benefit to an island country from some kinds of tourism development may thus be small indeed. Other kinds of tourist facilities provided by villages or financed locally may be economically more interesting.

The social impacts of tourism may also be important. Most jobs for local people in the tourist industry are as servants, house maids, waiters, gardeners and other menial work that may give people a sense of inferiority. At the same time the tourists come from other societies with different values and lifestyles, and because they have come seeking pleasure, they may spend large amounts of money and behave in ways that even they would not accept at home. Local people seeing the tourist example may want to live and behave the same way. Tourists may also, out of ignorance or carelessness, fail to respect local customs and moral values. These and other social effects may be among the most important long-term impacts of tourism development.

Environmental Impacts of Tourism Facilities

Tourism development usually starts with the construction of hotels, resorts and other places for tourists to stay. In addition there may be restaurants, night clubs, and recreation facilities such as golf courses, tennis courts, swimming pools, and marinas. These facilities require a lot of space, and land is usually scarce on an island. Land and resources used for tourism are not available for other uses; developers may even want to keep local people away from beaches, reefs and lagoon areas reserved for tourists only. Whenever possible, tourism developers prefer to build on the coast, where the hotel will front on a beach and perhaps a coral reef, yet the coast is the most fragile and vulnerable area on an island, with the greatest conflicts between uses.

The construction of these facilities can have the same kinds of impacts as any other construction projects, such as soil erosion, changes in water runoff, and damage to natural environments. If the resort is on the coast, the plans frequently call for changes in the coastline, such as the creation or improvement of a beach, the construction of an artificial island, or the dredging of a harbour or building of a dock for tour boats to use to pick up and leave off the tourists. These changes may upset normal coastal processes and be very difficult to maintain. Coastal hotel sites themselves are often vulnerable to storm damage, erosion and other problems because of their exposed location.

Tourist developments also require resources that may be scarce on an island. Water may be in short supply, yet tourist use of water is usually much greater per person than among the local population. Tourists require large quantities of high quality food; if it cannot be produced locally, it will have to be imported.

The sewage from large hotels can be a source of pollution if it is not treated and disposed of carefully. Most hotel projects include waste water treatment plants, but these can be difficult to maintain in the islands and need to be monitored regularly. Tourist facilities also produce large amounts of solid waste which can add to the existing solid waste disposal problems on many islands.

Infrastructure Requirements

Any major tourist development requires a good airport where large jets can bring tourists from overseas countries. Visits by tour ships may require improved docking facilities. Roads may have to be built to resort sites, or improved for tour buses. Water and electricity supplies may have to be increased. All these kinds of infrastructure require investments which must be added on to the direct cost of a tourism project.

Building roads, airports and docks can have major environmental impacts which are beyond the scope of this unit. Their overall effects, however, may be positive as well as negative. Such facilities benefit local people as well as tourists, reducing the isolation of remote areas and increasing the convenience of travel within the country and overseas. Tourism development can thus support useful expenditures that could not be justified for the local people alone.

Damage from Tourist Use

Tourists are often unaware of how fragile some island environments are. They may trample vegetation and thus cause erosion, or disturb birds and wildlife. They may leave their rubbish behind, littering the environment. They are apt to break corals as the walk or swim over the reef. Even anchoring in a fragile reef area can result in significant damage to corals. Tourists love to collect corals, shells and other pretty objects as souvenirs, but too much collecting can damage a reef or other site. Fishing is sport for a tourist, but it may take away resources needed as food in nearby villages.

Where a few tourists may do little damage, thousands of them can be a disaster. Think of the difference between one tourist breaking off a piece of coral, and hundreds of tourists each taking a piece of coral; a reef could quickly be stripped of its corals and shells. Areas subject to heavy tourist pressure should be protected from damaging activities. Laws may be needed to protect wildlife and to control collecting. The increasing demand for curios such as stuffed turtles, turtle shell jewelry, mounted butterflies, and traditional objects made with rare bird feathers or animal skins can threaten rare species with extinction. The manufacture and sale of such objects should be prohibited or strictly controlled. Coral, shells for handicrafts or collectors, and local trees used for carving can also be wiped out locally or reduced to low levels when too much is used to supply the tourist trade.

Planning Tourism Development

One major question to be answered in planning tourism development is what scale of tourism is appropriate for the local environment and culture. Every place has a carrying capacity that cannot be exceeded without bringing about serious changes or even the collapse of important resources or systems. While some small-scale tourism can be fit in almost anywhere, large scale tourism can cause major problems if it is not planned very carefully.

The number of tourists an area can absorb should be decided before tourism development goes to far, because there always will be pressures for bigger and bigger developments. The appropriate scale of tourism may be determined by the most limited resource, such as water or coastal land, or by the desire to prevent serious social or cultural impacts. How many people, for instance, can a community receive comfortably as visitors, or how would it feel to be outnumbered by the tourists on your own island?

It is therefore in the interest of the tourist industry to see that the overall planning of the country's development includes the requirements of tourism. As more governments begin environmental planning and make physical plans (including town plans, master plans and coastal zone plans), it is essential that these plans include the sites of particular scenic or recreational potential. The coastlines, vistas, swimming beaches, waterfalls, mountains and lagoons that tourists visit and photograph are capital assets just like hotels, but they are generally not owned by the tourism interests that benefit from them. Only careful comprehensive planning, and often the understanding and support of the traditional owners, can protect these resources from degradation and destruction.

In principle, planning helps in making choices between conflicting uses, or in finding ways to make them compatible. It should aim to locate unsightly or polluting activities, like industrial areas, fuel storage depots, rubbish dumps, etc., where they will not destroy the beauty of a town or coastline or conflict with tourist sites. In many island towns, there are already too many cases where urban pollution is making tourist beaches unsightly or unsafe. Planning early for tourism development can help to avoid damaging and expensive errors and also to prevent the gradual erosion of environmental values significant to tourism.

Improvements that help tourism, like better transportation, tree planting, restoration of historic sites, urban beautification and cleanliness, also improve the environment for the local population. Tourism development can help to stimulate general community improvement.

Conservation

One area where tourism interest coincides with the long term interest of a country is in the conservation of nature and traditional culture. Tourists are particularly attracted by unusual vegetation, birds and wildlife, by coral reefs and lagoons, and by distinctive cultures, customs and life styles. Very little has been done to develop these resources for better tourism, and ways need to be found to make them available without putting them at risk or degrading them.

The development of protected areas such as national parks and reserves can be one way to protect a country's heritage and to make it available for local education and tourism. The investment in facilities such as trails, signs, picnic shelters and visitors' centres is usually repaid through tourists who come in larger numbers and stay longer because there are more things to see and do.

Conservation areas will also attract special categories of tourists with interests in botany, bird watching, wildlife, nature photography, skin diving, archaeology, etc. Such kinds of tourists are generally more interested in the country they visit and less apt to cause serious social impacts.

Overall, tourism tends to be a mixed blessing in its benefits and impacts on the environment of destination locale. If it is allowed to grow unplanned, it can have serious social and environmental impacts while providing little real economic benefit. If developed with care, it can bring many advantages to small island communities with few other resources.

As such emerged the need of code of ethics and code of conduct for tourism industry.

Here in this book we have reproduced some such select codes with universal or general appeal and acceptability.

Role of International Associations in Sustainable Tourism Planning

WTO is developing the European Union's Blue Flag standard for coastal quality as a model for application worldwide. In addition, it has produced a guide book to help local planners develop appropriate planning mechanisms and manage tourism effectively. In the field of accommodation International Hotel Association (IHA) assist hoteliers to reconcile environmental issues with competitive pressures through the production of guidelines and information on environmental auditing from time to time. It imposes self-regulation and avoid government regulation. It promotes the financial benefits of integrating environmental measures in hotels at the construction stage. IHA has developed and promoted Twelve Environmental Resolutions for the Hotel Industry (based on WTC's Recommended Environmental Guidelines) and hosts the Annual International Hotels Association Environment Award (sponsored by American Express International). It has also prepared a policy paper on tourism and the environment with the European Tourism Action Group (ETAG), study of environmentally sound design and siting of hotels (with UNEP and WTO), and a guide to environmental auditing of small and medium sized hotels.

International Hotels Environment Initiative (IHEI) is another important organisation of 11 international hotel companies to guide the development of the programme and to foster the continual upgrading of environmental performance in the hotel industry worldwide. American Society of Travel Agents (ASTA) environment Committee is also developing programmes for members dealing with adventure travel and its relation to ecotourism. It has promoted environmentally compatible forms of travel and ensure that endangered and over-stressed travel areas are preserved for the enjoyment of future generations. ASTA's 'Guidelines for Responsible Environmental Travel' have been issued to millions of travellers, operators, and destinations. In addition, members subscribe to an environmental code as it has established the Annual ASTA/Smithsonian Magaxine Award for environmental excellence in the Travel and Tourism industry.

An international environmental seminar titled 'Protecting the Environment: Tourism Responsibility and Profitability' was organised in India in 1994 in cooperation with the Indian Government. It is likely to be repeated in other areas of the World in near future. Australian Tourism Industry Association (ATIA) is a representative association for the Travel & Tourism industry in Australia concerned with all aspects of tourism development in public and private sectors. It has developed environmental Policy to conserve and protect Australia's unique environment as the essential basis for the long-term success of the tourism industry. ATIA has developed and promoted the 'Code of Environmental Practice for the Tourism Industry'. As a part of the Prime Minister's Tourism Working Group, it participates in programmes on issues which may influence tourism development.. International Chamber of Commerce (ICC) also helps Travel and Tourism businesses around the World and improve its environmental performance. It produced the Business Charter for Sustainable Development in 1991 which is the basis for many other codes of conduct and recently (1993) established the World Industry Council for the Environment (WICE) to advise governments on environmental issues as they affect business and promote sound environmental management in companies.

International Air Transport Association's (IATA) Environmental Task Force (ETAF) has been concentrating on communicating the role of civil aviation in bringing about environmental protection tourist transit visitors over the last 20 years. ETAF's priorities in 1993 were to work toward minimixing unnecessary and impractical environmental restriction, to encourage fleet renewal and further reduction in airlines' environmental impacts, and to review the strategic responses required to meet the environmental challenges of the coming decade. International Federation of Tour Operators (IFTO) has established methods of assessing the impacts of tourism on the environment and guidelines for sustainable development. IFTO's regular meetings with national and regional governments, hoteliers and local tourist handling agents are used to promote environmentally sensitive policies for tourism development. In 1992, IFTO obtained funding from the European Community and the Spanish Government for the development of models and methodologies for sustainable tourism under ECOMOST Project.

This study had started in Mallorca and tested in Rhodes during 1993. From 1994, IFTO, with its partners, has been explaining how these models and methodologies can be put into practice in all resort areas, both in the European Community and Worldwide. IFTO will continue to promote environmental awareness amongst public and private sectors of the tourism industry as well as tourists. The largest tour operators in Europe, TUI and Thomson both of which are members of IFTO, are very active in the environmental field, improving environmental performance as well as printing environmental information in all of their brochures.

International Union for the Conservation of Nature—World Conservation Union (IUCN) has continued to develop its Environmental Law programme. In 1993, through the environmental law development component of the 'Programme, the final version draft of the International Covenant on Environment and Development was completed. IUCN provides advice and technical legal assistance to the governments of developing countries on request; publishes papers on relevant issues and sponsors regional conferences. In 1992, IUCN hosted the Fourth World Congress on National Parks and Protected Areas which produced the Caracas Declaration and an action plan entitled 'Parks for Life'. The third working group met to discuss the Draft Covenant for

Environmental Conservation and Sustainable Natural Resources, including the obligations laid out in AGENDA 21 and the Rio Declaration. In collaboration with the International Council on Environmental Law (ICEL) and WTTC, IUCN held a meeting of senior legal experts on the 'Protection of Cultural and Natural Heritage in Times of Armed Conflict'. United Nations Environment Programme has a Industry and Environment Programme Activity Centre (UNEP IE/PAC).

UNEP is a UN body responsible for environmental issues and representing the interests of the international community. It provides a platform to bring industry, government and NGOs together to work towards environmentally sound forms of industrial development. To this end, UNEP IE/PAC seeks to help formulate policies and strategies for sustainable industrial and tourism development, to facilitate their improvement and to stimulate the exchange of information. Its Key Activities/Achievements is to prepare technical reports, publications, workshops, seminars and forums, training and demonstration projects. In collaboration with other international associations, it developed AGENDA 21 programmes to promote environmentally sound activities industry wide. Recent activities include a technical report on 'The Development of National Parks and Protected Areas for Tourism', a joint programme with UNESCO and WTO on tourism and the environment in world heritage sites, and publication of an issue on 'Sustainable Tourism Development' of the Industry and Environment review.

World Travel and Tourism Council (WTTC) is a global coalition of chief executive officers from all sectors of Travel and Tourism, including transportation, accommodation, catering, recreational/cultural, and travel service activities. It ensures that national and international policies appropriately reflect the scale and importance of the Travel and Tourism industry and, through the Environment Research Centre, to promote environmentally compatible growth in the industry. Based on its business Charter for Sustainable Development, it developed and promoted Environmental Guidelines for Travel and Tourism companies.

In collaboration with the International Council on Environmental Law (ICEL) and- IUCN it held a meeting of senior legal experts on the Protection of Cultural and Natural Heritage in times of armed conflict. It developed research into the contribution of Travel and Tourism to the economy and produced a comprehensive report. It launched a research programme on the perception of Travel and Tourism in the world economy. It campaigns to improve tourism infrastructure globally and eliminate barriers to travel. WTTC will increase its efforts to promote environmentally compatible growth on the basis of management commitment, research and enlightened regulation. Pacific Asia Travel Association (PATA) has launched a new PATA award scheme, called 'Green Leaf. It designed to encourage good environmental behaviour by all suppliers of Travel and Tourism products and services as well as the use of environmental purchase criteria by consumers. This programme is based on PATA's 'Code for Environmentally Responsible Tourism' (CERT), promulgated in 1992 and the details of PATA's Code for Environmentally Responsible Tourism is as follows:

- ADOPT the necessary practices to conserve the environment, including the use of renewable resources in a sustainable manner and the conservation of non-renewable resources;
- CONTRIBUTE to the conservation of any habitat of flora and fauna, and of any site whether natural or cultural, which may be affected by tourism;
- ENCOURAGE relevant authorities to identify areas worthy of conservation and to determine the level of development, if any, which would ensure those areas are conserved;
- ENSURE that environmental assessment becomes

an integral step in the consideration of any site for a tourism project;

— COMPLY with all international, conventions in relation to the environment;

— COMPLY with all national, state, and local laws in relation to the environment;

— ENCOURAGE those involved in tourism comply with local, regional, and national planning policies and to participate in the planning process;

— PROVIDE the opportunity for the wider community to take part in discussions and consultations on tourism planning issues in so far as they affect the tourism industry and the community;

— ACKNOWLEDGE responsibility for the environmental impacts of all tourism related projects and activities and undertake all necessary responsible, remedial, and corrective actions;

— ENCOURAGE regular environmental audits of practices throughout the tourism industry and encourage necessary changes to those practices;

— FOSTER environmentally responsible practices, including waste management, recycling, and energy use;

— FOSTER, in both management and staff of all tourism-related projects and activities, an awareness of environmental and conservation principles;

— SUPPORT the inclusion of professional conservation principles in tourism education, training, and planning;

— ENCOURAGE an understanding by all those involved in tourism of each community's customs, cultural values, beliefs and traditions, and how they relate to the environment;

— ENHANCE the appreciation and understanding by tourists of the environment through the provision of accurate information and appropriate interpretation; and

— ESTABLISH detailed environmental policies and/or guidelines for the various sectors of the tourism industry.

The International Civil Aviation Environment organisation's Committee on Aviation Environmental Protection (CAEP) substantially revised its work programme in 1992 to place particular emphasis on determining the contribution of engine emission to problems in the upper atmosphere and to identify appropriate solutions to these problems. Its-aim and objective is to develop and promote environmentally responsible practices within the air transport industry in cooperation with other international bodies. ICAO is additionally concerned with establishing noise and emission standards for aircraft. ICAO has responsibility for the development of international guidelines and environmental standards for aircraft operations.

In 1990, it developed a worldwide policy Aviation Environmental Protection-Whose work programme was substantially revised in 1992 to give increased—emphasis to the impact of civil aviation on the upper atmosphere. Lufthansa, German Airlines, has developed a range of self-regulatory initiatives to minimise the impacts of its operations on the environment, employing the latest technology while instilling a sense of environmental responsibility among all personnel. The Chairman of the Executive Board, stated that "acceptance of responsibility for the environment is as much a part of the company's objectives as maintaining good customer relations or being competitive in the market". Lufthansa has frequently taken action in specific areas well ahead of regulatory requirements: For example, the company has invested in a younger fleet to reduce noise and gaseous pollutants.

The average age of the Lufthansa fleet is now less than six years, making it one of the world's youngest. The company has also invested in research to replace environmentally hazardous techniques or substances. Some companies, such as British Airways, run schemes to award environmental achievements within the company. Thailand-based Siam City Hotels & Resorts holds competitions for environmental ideas from employees, for example, a contest for 'green cartoons'. Qantas, for example, shows in-flight videos, developed with the cooperation of World Wide Fund for Nature (WWF), highlighting the problems generated by purchasing souvenirs made from the hides, tusks, horns and shells of endangered species of animals. Thomson Tour Operators has put environmental information into brouchures and trained representatives at resorts in using environmentally sound products. East Japan Railway Company has been striving to maintain a pleasant environment along its routes. Since 1992, 30,000 seedlings a year have been planted by company members and people living alongside the company's railways. British Airways Holidays has produced environmental destination guides for Thailand, Kenya and the Caribbean and offers customers the opportunity to donate, with a supporting donation from the company, to conservation projects endorsed by IUCN.

Travel & Tourism companies can also play an important role in conserving resources through communication and education initiatives. Japan Travel Bureau, Japan's leading tour operator, organised a tour of Malaysia's tropical rain forest to show the damage that had been done and to raise support for a reforestation scheme. American Airlines encourages corporate staff and family involvement in the enhancement of the environment. KLM Royal Dutch Airlines is reducing the number of private cars driving to Schipol airport by developing more efficient public transport. East Japan Railway Company has encouraged passengers *to* support its recycling programme by placing separate bins for bottles and cans, newspapers and magazines, and other waste in stations. This has made it possible to reduce the amount of waste produced each year by roughly half. Asilomar State Beach and Conference Grounds in the USA have replanted thousands of native dune species, and presented more than 1,200 interpretive programmes to over 40,000 clients emphasising the importance of preserving local flora and fauna.

Coming to case of India, despite known for sustainable development approach right from the time of the Mauryas, when we had introduced do's and don'ts for *Abhyaranyas* (Parks), could not plan and control natural resources of the country systematically. We frame rules and regulations for sustainable development of tourist places but could not implement respective guidelines and development evaluation standards. Goa is perhaps the only state which is highly conscious of the need to maintain and preserve nature, ecology and Environment protection act, 1986, enforced by the Union Ministry of Environment and Forests through its notification issued in February, 1991.

The development needs to be monitored carefully lest they are in danger of environment damage that is irreversible. The Konkan railway project in the Western Ghats is on completion and needs precautionary measures before it got delayed. Western Ghats are unique both naturally and geologically. The Ghats are the system of land elevation, hills, mountains, plateaus and dotted with beautiful sea beaches from Bombay to Kanyakumari. Bombay is the entry point of foreign tourist arrivals. But, after economic liberalisation in 1991, the occupancy rate of accommodation units increased and Bombay city has started to cater more number of tourists than ever. Exceeding pressures of increased commercial units and increased migration of people, Mumbai has deteriorated both its land and coasts due to over exploitation of natural resources.

A number of proposals have been made for the protection of flora and fauna and restoration of lakes, fountains and streams in the Himalaya. But it is noticed that a fairly large number of valleys, meaows, slopes, glaciers and forests are loosing their existence, serenity and culture day by day as mass influx of visitors have not only created the problem of carrying capacity but increased the possibilities of social and visual pollution and ruthless duploitation. HIMTAB organises Mountain Tourism meets inside of Hotel Complexes is required to take subject experts to such destinations which have been severely affected by man-made and physical onslauguts. There is lack of Coordination with local people as we do not find active participation of *Gram-Pradhans* and local Social Workers in the planning and management of tourist places. Development parametres and tourism measurement methods should be applied on destination wise not for the entire Himalaya as a whole.

The lakes of India, require careful planning from all concerned. The role of Planning Commission is commendable as it has recommended that the National Lake Conservation Plan (NLCP) be considered a centrally sponsored scheme in the ninth plan, with all the funds being provided by the centre. The eleven lakes out of twenty one lakes covered for this purpose are Dal (J&K), Sukhna (Chandigarh), Sagar and Bhoj (M.P.), Nainital (Uttaranchal), Kodai Kanal, Ooty (Tamil Nadu), Rabindra Sagar (West Bengal), Powai (Maharashtra), Udaipur lakes (Rajasthan) and Hussain Sagar (Andhra Pradesh). The Andhra Government is also planning to entrust private parties with the beautification of Hussain Sagar lake and developing it as a tourist spot. India's historic monuments and cultural sites are internationally known. But most of the architecturally rich centres are not renovated because of lack of funds. Environmental degradation, industrial pollution and illegal encroachments have taken their toll where efforts have been made at conservation the results have been crude and insenstive.

However, the efforts of Delhi Government to hand over some historical monuments here for preservation and upkeep to business houses is appreciatable. The Rajasthan Government has also taken initiative in this field as the Archaeological Survey of India probably did not pay more attention on historic buildings richly carved by marvels. But one factor which has had a lasting impact on the process of conservation is the lack of Coordination between the Ministry of Tourism and the Ministry of Culture. While the former still adheres to the old ASI approach, the Ministry of Tourism has adopted a revenue generating approach. But things are changing now for the better.

2

WTO Recommendations to Government for Supporting and/or Establishing National Certification Systems for Sustainable Tourism

Certification systems for sustainable tourism play an increasing role in regulating tourism operations as voluntary instruments above legal frameworks. They usually address three main aspects, namely: 1) environmental performance of companies, operations and destinations; 2) product quality; and 3) corporate social responsibility of operations. They normally target tourism suppliers, such as accommodation, restaurants, sport and leisure facilities, tourist attractions, destinations, tour operators, (tourist) transport companies, tourist associations, etc.

Considering the growing number and importance of certification systems and other voluntary initiatives in tourism, and based on a recommendation made by the UN Commission on Sustainable Development, WTO undertook a comprehensive worldwide study on this topic. The results of this study were published in 2002, under the title "Voluntary Initiatives for Sustainable Tourism: Worldwide Inventory and Comparative Analysis of 104 Eco-labels, Awards And Self-commitments".

The WTO Committee on Sustainable Development of Tourism, at its 3rd Session held in Costa Rica, 25-26 September 2002 recommended the preparation of a set of guidelines for Governments on certification systems for sustainable tourism. Acting on this decision of the Committee, the present document aims at enhancing awareness among governments about the opportunities certification systems may provide as part of their sustainable development policy goals, and provides basic recommendations for supporting and/or establishing such systems at the national level. It is primarily based on the WTO study mentioned above. It also draws on the survey conducted among WTO Member States in November 2001-January 2002, considering the feasibility of a Sustainable Tourism Stewardship Council, on the experience gained in the area of certification through the International Year of Ecotourism 2002, on comments received from the Committee members, and on other relevant documents.

The Role of Governments in Present Certification Systems

The WTO study on voluntary initiatives for sustainable tourism revealed that governments have an important role in many of the certification systems presently operating. Twenty of the 59 certification schemes investigated are lead by government agencies. A further 18 have government involvement, either through direct financial support, marketing support, expert know-how in criteria setting, verification procedures, or surveillance of procedures followed by the certification body. Government financial support is crucial to half the schemes for which data is available. Government agencies involved generally include either environment ministries, national tourism authorities and tourist boards, and in fewer cases, standards institutes.

Certification systems can bring benefits to society, the environment, governments, private companies and consumers as well.

Potential benefits for society:

— Generally speaking, societies will benefit from certification systems that cover the three aspects of sustainability: social, environmental and economic. Certified companies are supposed to generate benefits in these three areas, while reducing their negative impacts. Therefore, the contribution of tourism activities to the sustainable development of host societies will be more evident, more measurable and more accountable.

— Furthermore, the level of awareness on sustainability issues will be stronger in the host society if the large majority of tourism companies and/or destinations are certified.

Potential benefits for the environment:

— It is evident that certification systems and ecolabels that include strict environmental criteria result in benefits for the local environment and, to the extent that some mass tourism activities can impact biodiversity and climate change, also the global environment.

— Furthermore, the widespread use of ecolabels and certification systems in the tourism industry helps to generate increased environmental awareness among both, tourists and host societies and should result in more caring attitudes with respect to the natural and built environments.

Potential benefits for governments:

— Providing an effective alternative to direct regulation, which could prove more difficult and time-consuming to implement;

— Enabling governments to adopt a flexible approach to monitoring the tourism industry, permitting organisations to proceed at the pace they feel most comfortable with, while encouraging them to develop innovative approaches to environmental and socio-cultural improvements;
— Giving tourism companies greater scope for making environmental and social improvements by exploiting opportunities specific to their individual circumstances, rather than governments having to control and inspect companies in order to check that they comply with general, industry-wide regulations;
— Allowing part of the costs of implementing and monitoring environmental protection measures to be transferred to the industry itself, thereby reducing the financial burden of regulation on the taxpayer;
— National programmes of tourism certification can enhance tourism's recognition in the country, national competitiveness and image in international markets.

Potential benefits for companies:

— Adherence to voluntary environmental initiatives can enable the company to market its products more effectively, and to improve their public image among consumers, business partners and with the host communities;
— Engaging in voluntary certification can help companies to signal their specific commitment to environmental, social and even economic improvements, which may in turn help to defer the need for further direct regulation by governments;

— Pursuing sound environmental management strategies can generate substantial cost savings for the company;

— Participation in a certification programme can provide better access to modern techniques, technology and know-how;

— Applying effective environmental management can help to protect the environmental and cultural assets upon which the tourism industry depends for its continued prosperity.

Finally, certification and ecolabels can of course benefit consumers by providing them with more information and guidance for their decisions on travel choices, as well as assurances for product and service quality.

Recommendations

Certification systems for sustainable tourism need to be developed and operated to fit geographical, political, socio-economic and sectoral characteristics of each country. For this reason, the following recommendations serve as general orientation and they need to be adapted to the economic, institutional, social and environmental conditions prevailing in each country.

1. Development of the Certification System

Governments can play a key role in the initiation and development of certification systems for sustainable tourism by creating the supportive legal and institutional structures. The following general recommendations can be made:

1. Consider a national certification system as an integral part of sustainable tourism development policies, strategies and objectives, and an effective tool to implement them.
2. Identify key stakeholders and potential target groups

relevant to and interested in certification programmes.

3. Develop the certification system through multi-stakeholder consultation processes, involving all relevant interest groups, such us different government authorities (tourism, environment, transportation, finance, education, etc); tourism trade associations and other private groups; academic, education and research institutions; NGOs; consumer associations; etc. The development and the operation of a successful certification programme in many cases lays in the multi-stakeholder representation of the team awarding certificates and supporting the programme.

4. Coordinate an in-depth research on the conditions and feasibility of a certification system, including aspects such as:
   - Existing legal and voluntary instruments affecting the tourism sector (e.g. laws, regulations, taxes, subsidies, local certification systems, codes of conduct, environmental awards, etc.);
   - Experience of certification systems applied in other sectors in the country, like agriculture, forestry, and draw lessons from them for the tourism sector
   - Certification criteria (see section 2 below);
   - Operational mechanisms: application, verification, awarding, revision and inspection procedures; consulting and technical assistance for participants, marketing and communication; funding (see section 3).

5. Provide finance and/or seek partners for co-financing and providing technical contributions for the research, development and operational costs

of certification programmes (e.g. different government departments, NGOs, academic institutions, international finance and development agencies, private foundations, etc).

6. Ensure transparency throughout all the stages of the development and operation of the certification system and establish an appeals process.
7. Make clear to the private sector the benefits, costs and other implications of certification systems.
8. Develop incentives to motivate and encourage tourism companies to become certified, e.g. marketing incentives by giving priority in trade shows and nationally sponsored publicity, or ensuring access to environmental technologies, etc.
9. Consider issues affecting the sustainability of destinations as a whole, involving all tourism product and service providers.
10. Pay special attention to equitable access to certification, especially by small and medium size firms, as they can have more difficulties in meeting the costs and technical requirements than bigger companies.
11. Conduct pilot projects for testing and demonstration of the certification system.
12. Prepare the market for certification, in order to reach a good demand level from tourism companies, and a critical mass at the initial phase to get the system running.

2. Certification Criteria

Developing certification criteria is a critical part of the certification system development process. The following general recommendations need to be considered:

1. Base criteria on existing legal standards and instruments and set them well above legal compliance.
2. Include the precondition of compliance by the applicant with these legislations.
3. Address the three dimensions of sustainability: environmental, socio-cultural and economic issues.
4. Define core criteria and supplementary criteria specific for different tourism product and service groups (e.g. hotels and other accommodations, transportation services, restaurants, tour operators and travel agents, attractions, etc.). By this way consider the implications to destinations as a whole, and not just certain tourism product and service groups.
5. In bigger countries, criteria can be adjusted to specific regional and local environmental and socio-economic conditions.
6. For each criterion, define indicators that are measurable and easy to understand by the different type of stakeholders involved in the certification process.
7. Base criteria and indicators on scientific research that evaluates the key environmental and socio-economic impacts of the sector.
8. Criteria should refer to attainable and realistic goals for private sector participants.
9. Criteria can be set in different levels of requirements: from more easily achievable to very demanding criteria. Thus, the certification system sets a framework for continuous improvement whereby applicants can achieve higher performance levels step by step.

10. Compliance with criteria can be measured through process and performance-based assessments. Indicators are essential tools for measuring environmental, social and economic impacts of tourism operations:

    Environmental indicators can relate to the following factors, among others:

- Environmental impact assessment conducted for setting up the operation or construction of establishments;
- Environmental management practices, company policies and technical measures (e.g. energy, water saving and waste treatment devices, environmental friendly transportation, etc.) in place;
- Land use and property issues in destinations;
- Health and safety;
- Use of natural resources:
  - Energy (consumption, reduction, efficiency)
  - Water (consumption, reduction, quality)
  - Solid and liquid waste (reduction, reuse, recycling, treatment, disposal)
  - Appropriate building materials
  - Hazardous substances (reduction, handling, use of nature friendly cleaning products)
  - Noise (reduction)
  - Air quality (quality, improvement)
  - Habitat/eco-system/wildlife maintenance and enhancement;
- Environmental information/interpretation/education for customers;
- Transportation services (public transport, environmental friendly alternatives;

— Indicators and standards on the impacts at specific tourist use areas (e.g. beaches) and on the impacts caused by specific tourism activities and facilities (e.g. diving, golf, marinas etc.);
— Visual impacts of establishments and infrastructure; etc.

Social indicators can relate to the following factors, among others:

— Social impact assessment conducted for setting up the operation and the establishments;
— Staff policies and management (information, education, training, incentives, health, safety, etc.);
— Relationships with local communities (local employees, outreach and education programmes);
— Emphasis on, and conservation of local/regional culture, heritage and authenticity;
— Maintaining aesthetics of physical development/architecture;
— Community feedback systems, satisfaction of local population;
— Contribution to community development purposes (infrastructure improvement; social services, etc.);
— Information provided to guests on sustainability aspects;
— Guest feedback systems in place, customer satisfaction, etc.

Economic indicators can relate to the following factors, among others:

— Creation of local employment (number of employees from local communities and their level of skills);
— Supply chain management through green and sustainable purchasing policies;

— Creation of networks of environmentally friendly businesses within a given destination;
— Responsible marketing;
— Use of locally sourced and produced materials and food, etc.

In addition, certification criteria for ecotourism should specifically address the elements below, besides the general sustainability criteria:

— Financial and in-kind contributions to conservation of ecotourism sites by companies;
— Level of involvement of local communities and benefits accruing to them;
— Use of specialised guides and other interpretation techniques, information provided to tourists through ecotourism operations;
— Environmental education activities provided for tourists and local populations;
— Locally appropriate scale and design for lodging, infrastructure and tours;
— Minimal impact on and the appropriate presentation of local and indigenous culture.

11. Indicators to measure the success of certification systems can address:

— The number of applications and certified companies (i.e. increase over time of the number of companies registered in a certain certification system);
— The percentage of certified companies in the different tourism product and service groups;
— Improvement in environmental and social performance in certified companies (e.g. changes in water and energy consumption, resource savings, etc.);

— Environmental and social performance of certified companies as compared to non-certified ones (e.g. a current estimate is that environmental performance per certified accommodation enterprises can be taken as about 20 % better than the average performance at accommodation facilities in Europe).

12. Consider the whole product life cycle when setting product environmental criteria (from the manufacturing, transporting, through purchasing, consumption, to recycling, disposal, etc.).
13. Undertake periodic revision and update of criteria (e.g. every 2-3 years).

3. Operation of Certification Systems

The procedure is normally composed of the application, verification and certification processes. The funding mechanism for the above services and procedures is a crucial and critical element for the success of certification systems. Normally there is a funding, verification and certification body interacting in these processes. In many cases the funding and certification bodies coincide. Fundamental components of any certification system are the facilitation of consulting, advisory and technical assistance and marketing services. The following general recommendations can be made in relation to the operational processes:

3.1 Application

1. The system should be open to all potential applicants.
2. Provide clear and easily accessible information on the criteria, costs and benefits and other conditions of certification (e.g. through Internet, email, telephone, information kit).
3. Offer immediate sources for consultation services.
4. Show tangible benefits for applicants (e.g. costs

savings, marketing advantage, access to technical assistance and modern technology and financial possibilities, etc.) and explain clearly the commitments and costs.

5. Application documents should be clear, easy to understand and fill in.
6. Conduct a pre-evaluation/assessment of the applicant in order to identify technical and technological aspects that need to be improved to meet the criteria. Provide assistance and financial incentives for these improvements.

3.2 Verification

7. Verification of compliance with criteria should be done by an independent or third-party organisation. In other words by a body which is independent from the parties being certified and of technical assessment or funding.
8. Verification is normally done through a combination of different activities: review of application documents and references, self-assessment by the operation through questionnaire, on-site visit, fees to be paid by the applicant.
9. Verification audits should be conducted by suitably trained auditors.
10. The verification process can be also used to give recommendations to the applicants on how to improve their performance and achieve further progress.

3.3 Certification (awarding of certification)

The certification is basically the awarding of the certification to the applicant, granting a permit for using the logo, marketing and other services of the system.

11. Certification bodies can be composed of representatives of the mayor stakeholder groups participating in the development and operation of the system. Governments have a key role in certification bodies, by giving credibility and recognition of the system.
12. As it was also mentioned among the recommendations for criteria development, awarding of certification can be done at single-level or at multi-level. The latter one occurs if criteria are set on different scales with a view to ensure a framework of continuous improvement.
13. The certification, the use of a logo and related benefits should be granted for a pre-determined period, after which re-assessment and verification should be conducted to ensure continuous compliance with the same or higher criteria.
14. Follow up control can be conducted after certification. For example, the WTO study on voluntary initiatives demonstrated that more than 50% of the certification systems currently operating undertake some control visits after certification: 38% are announced, and 17% are surprise visits. Some eco-labels either do phone checks, stimulating guests' feedback or sending "mystery guests" to the certified tourism service.
15. Procedures have to be in place for the cancellation and withdrawal of certification and the use of the corresponding logo in case of non-compliance.
16. The certification system can also include consumer and local community feedback mechanisms.

3.4 Consulting, Advisory and Technical Assistance Services

The facilitation of the following services represents

important added value for tourism companies and can be decisive factors for joining the certification system.

17. Provide technical consultancy options from the initial expression of interest and through the application phases onward, and give guidance to the applicant at every stage of the process.
18. Facilitate technical assistance for applicants so that they can introduce advanced management techniques and technology to meet the certification criteria. Provide access to environmental technologies, equipments and techniques by creating alliances with other organisations that can provide assistance for this purpose.
19. Develop training and capacity building programmes in form of courses, workshops, distance learning, etc.
20. Organise regular meetings for certified companies to promote the exchange of experiences and the sense of group.
21. Constant assistance and advisory is especially important in certification systems where the criteria and awarding are set on different scales.

3.5 Marketing and Communication

Marketing is another fundamental element of certification programmes, representing perhaps the biggest attraction and the most tangible benefits for private companies. The following general recommendations can be made:

22. Develop a precise marketing strategy for the certification system targeting three groups in principle:

22a. Potential candidates: aiming at attracting companies to join the programme

22b. Applicants and certified companies: providing marketing and promotional support and market advantages for them

22c. Consumers: reaching recognition of the certification programmes, fostering responsible travel choices, and make effective the marketing advantage for certified companies.

23. Develop a well-distinguished and unequivocal logo design for the system. The logo can be accompanied by a motto, or slogan. Ensure legal protection of the logo.

24. The presentation of the system in media and communication should reflect a well recognised corporate image in the market for businesses and consumers as well. The system can represent a sort of brand.

25. Use all available forms and channels to publicise and provide information on the certification programme for companies and consumers (e.g. brochures, flyers, guide books, printed and electronic media, Internet, conferences, seminars, tourism and trade fairs, etc.)

26. Give good media coverage to the awarding ceremonies.

27. Provide marketing support and promotion for certified companies through national tourist boards or national tourism marketing organisations, e.g. presentation of these companies in national brochures, catalogues, listings, websites, support for presence at national stands at tourism fairs and exhibition, etc.

28. Give recommendations and examples to applicants and certified companies on how to include the certificate in their own marketing activities.

29. Demonstrate the distinction on environmental performance, economic and socio-cultural effects between certified and non-certified products/ companies.
30. Communicate on a regular basis with certified members (e.g. through periodic meetings and events, newsletters, emails, exclusive access to information on Internet, etc.)
31. Provide clear and easily understandable information to consumers on the characteristics and added value that certification represents.
32. Develop consumer awareness raising and education campaigns on the certification system and certified products.
33. Involve consumer associations in these efforts

3.6 Fees and Funding

Governments have a key role in providing funding themselves, and/or in conceiving and developing alternative funding mechanisms with other partners for the operation of the certification system.

34. Establish the right balance between financial contributions of the public and private sectors.
35. Ensure that the sources of funding do not create a conflict of interest, since undue influence by funding organisations should be avoided in the certification procedure.
36. Establish fees for participants to cover (at least part of) application and verification costs. Fees should be kept as low as possible in order to encourage participation.
37. Fees should be calculated proportionally to size of businesses (e.g. by number of beds or visitors, turnover, etc.).

38. Provide incentive measures and support the application of companies, especially of small and medium size enterprises that would otherwise be left out (e.g. by soft loans and subsidies to make the necessary improvements to meet the criteria).
39. Consider in-kind contributions by governments for the operation, e.g. providing facilities, office space and equipment.

Final Note: Governments are encouraged to convey to the World Tourism Organisation their experience in connection with certification systems related to sustainability in tourism. This will allow WTO to periodically revise these guidelines, introduce any additional guidelines or modify those recommended above (Madrid, March 2003).

3

Indian Tourism Act and Associated Policy Frameworks

TOURISM PROMOTION BILL

Be it enacted by Parliament in the Fifty-third Year of the Republic of India as follows:—

Short Title, Extent and Commencement

1. (1) This Act may be called the Tourism Promotion Act, 2002.

(2) It extends to the whole of India.

(3) It shall come into force on such date, as the Central Government may, by notification in the Official Gazette, appoint.

Definitions

2. In this Act, unless the context otherwise requires—

(a) "appropriate Government" means in case of a State, the Government of that State and in other cases, the Central Government;

(b) "Corporation" means the Tourism Promotion Corporation of India established under section 3;

(c) "Director-Genreal" means the Director-General of the Corporation; and

(d) "prescribed" means prescribed by rules made under this Act.

Establishment of Tourism Promotion Corporation of India

3. (1) The Central Government shall, by notification in the Official Gazette, establsih a Corporation to be known as Tourism Promotion Corporation of India with its headquarters at New Delhi.

(2) The Corporation may set up an office in the capital city of each State and Union Territory.

Composition of the Corporation

4. (1) The Corporation shall be headed by a Director-General and assisted by such number of Directors and Officers to be appointed by the Central Government as may be required for the efficient functioning of the Corporation.

(2) Each office of the Corporation shall be headed by a Director and shall consist of such number of officers and other staff as may be prescribed.

Functions of the Corporation

5. The Corporation shall perform the following functions, namely:—

(i) formulate a policy to promote tourism in the country as early as possible;

(ii) to give wide publicity to its policy and projects through electronic and print media;

(iii) to organize cultural functions at various tourist places at regular intervals with a view to creating awareness among the general, public and the visiting foreign tourists about the culture and tradition of people belonging to different regions of the country;

(iv) in co-ordination with Indian Embassy in each country, to organize cultural functions with a view to depicting our culture and tradition in that country;

(v) to take suitable measures for the promotion of interest of the foreign tourists in the country through a professional approach by providing suitable incentives and comforts to attract them.

Power to Make Rules

6. The Central Government may, by notification in the Official Gazette, make rules for carrying out the purposes of this Act.

Statement of Objects and Reasons

India is a large country having vast tourism potential. However, it has not been exploited fully to the advantage of the country. Every year lakhs of tourists visit our country from abroad. It is a known fact that the foreign tourists face a lot of hardships and unpleasant experience while they travel in our country. There are frequent complaints of the foreign tourists being cheated by middlemen, touts and others. They carry a bad impression about our country on their return. This hampers the flow of foreign tourists into our country.

2. India is a vast country having different cultures and traditions and various languages. People of one region are not aware of the culture and tradition of people belonging to other regions. As such they face a lot of difficulties while visiting important tourist places.

3. Therefore, it is proposed to set up a Tourism Promotion Corporation with a view to promote tourism in the country and attract foreign tourists in large numbers. It is also proposed to provide that the corporation shall function with professional approach in order to perform its functions effectively.

The Bill seeks to attain these objectives.

—P. Prabhakar Reddy

Financial Memorandum

Clause 3 of the Bill provides that the Central Government shall set up a corporation to be known as Tourism Promotion Corporation of India with its headquarters at New Delhi and an office in each State and Union Territory. Clause 4 provides that the corporation shall consist of a Director-General, Directors and Officers.

The Bill, therefore, if enacted will involve expenditure from the Consolidated Fund of India. It is likely to involve an annual recurring expenditure of rupees two hundred crore from the Consolidated Fund of India. A non-recurring expenditure of rupees two hundred crore is also likely to be involved.

Memorandum Regarding Delegated Legislation

Clause 6 of the Bill empowers the Central Government to make rules for carrying out the provisions of the Bill. As the rules will relate to matters of detail only, the delegation of legislative power is of a normal character.

BAGGAGE RULES, INDIA (1998)

Short Title and Commencement

(i) These rules may be called the Baggage Rules, 1998.

(ii) They shall come into force on the date of their publication in the Official Gazette.

Definitions

In these rules, unless the context otherwise requires,-

(i) "appendix" means an Appendix to these rules;

(ii) "resident" means a person holding a valid passport

issued under the Passports Act, 1967 (15 of 1967) and normally residing in India;

(iii) "tourist" means a person not normally resident in India, who enters India for a stay of not more than six months in the course of any twelve months period for legitimate non-immigrant purposes, such as touring, recreation, sports, health, family reasons, study, religious pilgrimage or business;

(iv) "family" includes all persons who are residing in the same house and form part of the same domestic establishment;

(v) "professional equipment" means such portable equipments, instruments, apparatus and appliances as are required in his profession, by a carpenter, a plumber, a welder, a mason, and the like and shall not include items of common use such as cameras, cassette recorders, dictaphones, personal computers, typewriters, and other similar articles.

Passengers returning from countries other than Nepal, Bhutan, Myanmar or China

An Indian resident or a foreigner residing in India, returning from any country other than Nepal, Bhutan, Myanmar or China, shall be allowed clearance free of duty articles in his bona fi*de* baggage to the extent mentioned in column (2) of Appendix A.

Provided that such Indian resident or such foreigner coming by land route as specified in Annexure IV, shall be allowed clearance free of duty articles in his bonafide baggage to the extent mentioned in column (2) of Appendix 'B'.

Passengers returning from Nepal, Bhutan, Myanmar or China

An Indian resident or a foreigner residing in India, returning from Nepal, Bhutan, Myanmar or China, other than by land route, shall be allowed clearance free of duty articles in his *bona fide* baggage to the extent mentioned in column (2) of Appendix B.

Professionals returning to India

An Indian passenger who was engaged in his profession abroad shall on his return to India be allowed clearance free of duty, in addition to what he is allowed under rule 3 or, as the case may be, under rule 4, articles in his *bona fide* baggage to the extent mentioned in column (2) of Appendix C.

Jewellery

A passenger returning to India shall be allowed clearance free of duty jewellery in his *bona fide* baggage to the extent mentioned in column (2) of Appendix D.

Tourists

A tourist arriving in India shall be allowed clearance free of duty articles in his *bona fide* baggage to the extent mentioned in column (2) of Appendix E.

Transfer of residence

(1) A person who is transferring his residence to India shall be allowed clearance free of duty, in addition to what he is allowed under rule 3 or, as the case may be, under rule 4, articles in his *bona fide* baggage to the extent mentioned in column (1) of Appendix F, subject to the conditions, if any, mentioned in the corresponding entry in column (2) of the said Appendix.

(2) The conditions may be relaxed to the extent mentioned in column (3) of the said Appendix.

Provisions regarding unaccompanied baggage

(1) Provisions of these Rules are also extended to unaccompanied baggage except where they have been specifically excluded.

(2) The unaccompanied baggage had been in the possession abroad of the passenger and is dispatched within one month of his arrival in India or within such further period as the Assistant Commissioner of Customs or Deputy Commissioner of Customs may allow.

(3) The unaccompanied baggage may land in India upto 2 months before the arrival of the passenger or within such period, not exceeding one year, as the Assistant Commissioner of Customs or Deputy Commissioner of Customs may allow, for reasons to be recorded, if he is satisfied that the passenger was prevented from arriving in India within the period of two months due to circumstances beyond his control such as sudden illness of the passenger or a member of his family, or natural calamities or disturbed conditions or disruption of the transport or travel arrangements in the country or countries concerned or any other reasons, which necessitated a change in the travel schedule of the passenger.

Application of these Rules to members of the crew

The provisions of these Rules shall apply in respect of members of the crew engaged in a foreign going vessel for importation of their baggage at the time of final pay off on termination of their engagement.

Provided that except as specified in this sub-rule, a crew member of a vessel shall be allowed to bring items like chocolates, cheese, cosmetics and other petty gift items for their personal or family use which shall not exceed the value of rupees six hundred.

(2) Notwithstanding anything contained in these rules a crew member of an aircraft shall be allowed to bring items like chocolates, cheese, cosmetics and other petty gift items at the time of the returning of the aircraft from foreign journey for their personal or family use which shall not exceed the value of rupees six hundred

Appendix A

(See rule 3)

(1) Articles allowed free of duty

(2) (a) All passengers of and above 10 years of age and returning after stay abroad of more than three days.

(i) Used personal effects, excluding jewellery, required for satisfying daily necessities of life.

(ii) Articles other than those mentioned in Annex. I upto a value of Rs. 25,000 if these are carried on the person or in the accompanied baggage of the passenger.

(b) All passengers of and above 10 years of age and returning after stay abroad of three days or less. (i) Used personal effects, excluding jewellery, required for satisfying daily necessities of life.

(ii) Articles other than those mentioned in Annex. I upto a value of Rs. 12,000 if these are carried on the person or in the accompanied baggage of the passenger.

(c) All passengers up to 10 years of age and returning after stay abroad of more than three days. (i) Used personal effects, excluding jewellery, required for satisfying daily necessities of life.

(ii) Articles other than those mentioned in Annex. I upto a value of Rs. 6,000 if these are carried on the person or in the accompanied baggage of the passenger.

(d) All passengers upto 10 years of age and returning after stay abroad of three days or less.

(i) Used personal effects, excluding jewellery, required for satisfying daily necessities of life.

(ii) Articles other than those mentioned in Annex. I upto a value of Rs. 3000 if these are carried on the person or in the accompanied baggage of the passenger.

Explanation. - The free allowance under this rule shall not be allowed to be pooled with the free allowance of any other passenger.

APPENDIX B

(See rule 4)

(1) (i) Passengers of and above 10 years of age and returning after stay abroad of more than three days.

(2) (i) Used personal effects, excluding jewellery, required for satisfying daily necessities of life.

(ii) Articles other than those mentioned in Annex. I upto a value of Rs. 6,000 if these are carried on the person or in the accompanied baggage of the passenger.

(ii) Passengers upto 10 years of age and returning after stay abroad of more than three days.

(3) (i) Used personal effects, excluding jewellery, required for satisfying daily necessities of life.

(ii) Articles other than those mentioned in Annex. I upto a value of Rs. 1500 if these are carried on the person or in the accompanied baggage of the passenger.

Explanation. - The free allowance under this rule shall not be allowed to be pooled with the free allowance of any other passenger.

Appendix C

(See rule 5)

(1) Articles allowed free of duty

(2) (a) Indian passenger returning after at least 3 months.

(i) Used household articles upto an aggregate value of Rs. 12,000

(ii) Professional equipment upto a value of Rs. 20,000..

(b) Indian passenger returning after at least 6 months.

(i) Used household articles upto an aggregate value of Rs.12,000

(ii) Professional equipment upto a value of Rs. 40,000.

(c) Indian passenger returning after a stay of minimum 365 days during the preceding 2 years on termination of his work, and who has not availed this concession in the preceding three years.

(i) Used household articles and personal effects, (which have been in the possession and use abroad of the passenger or his family for at least six months), and which are not mentioned in Annex I, Annex II or Annex. III upto an aggregate value of Rs.75,000.

Appendix D

(See rule 6)

(1) Jewellery

(2) Indian passenger who has been residing abroad for over one year.

(i) Jewellery upto an aggregate value of Rs. 10,000 by a gentleman passenger, or

(ii) Upto aggregate value of Rs. 20,000 by a lady passenger.

Appendix E

(See rule 7)

(1) Articles allowed free of duty (a) Tourists of Indian origin coming to India other than tourists of Indian origin coming by land routes as specified in Annexure IV

(i) used personal effects and travel souvenirs, if- (2) (a) these goods are for personal use of the tourist, and (b) these goods, other than those consumed during the stay in India, are re-exported when the tourist leaves India for a foreign destination.

(ii) articles as allowed to be cleared under rule 3 or rule 4.

(2) Tourists of foreign origin other than those of Nepalese origin coming from Nepal or of Bhutanese origin coming Bhutan or of Pakistani origin coming from Pakistan.

(i) used personal effects and travel souvenirs, if- (a) these goods are for personal use of the tourist, and (b) these goods, other than those consumed during the stay in India, are re-exported when the tourist leaves India for a foreign destination.

(ii) articles upto a value of Rs.8000 for making gifts.

(c) Tourists of Nepalese origin coming from Nepal or of Bhutanese origin coming from Bhutan. No free allowance.

(d) Tourists –

(i) of Pakistani origin coming from Pakistan other than by land routes;

(ii) of Pakistani origin or foreign tourists coming by land routes as specified in Annexure IV;

(iii) of Indian origin coming by land routes as specified in Annexure IV (i) used personal effects and travel souvenirs, if

(a) these goods are for personal use of the tourist, and

(b) these goods, other than those consumed during the stay in India, are re-exported when the tourist leaves India for a foreign destination.

(ii) articles upto a value of Rs.6000 for making gifts.

Appendix F

(a) Used personal and household articles, other than those listed at Annex. I or Annex. II, but including jewellery upto ten thousand rupees by a gentleman passenger or rupees twenty thousand by a lady passenger.

(i) Minimum stay of two years abroad, immediately preceding the date of his arrival on TR,
(ii) total stay in India on short visit during the 2 preceding years should not exceed 6 months, and
(iii) passenger has not availed this concession in the preceding three years.

(a) For condition (1) Shortfall of upto 2 months in stay abroad can be condoned by Assistant Commissioner of Customs or Deputy Commissioner of Customs if the early return is on account of :

(i) terminal leave or vacation being availed of by the passenger; or
(ii) any other special circumstances. (b) For condition (2)

Commissioner of Customs may condone short visits in excess of 6 months in deserving cases. (c) For condition (3) No relaxation (b) Jewellery taken out earlier by the passenger or by a member of his family from India. Satisfaction of the Asstt. Commissioner of Customs regarding the jewellery having been taken out earlier from India.

Annex I

1. Firearms.
2. Cartridges of fire arms exceeding 50.
3. Cigarettes exceeding 200 or cigars exceeding 50 or tobacco exceeding 250 gms.
4. Alcoholic liquor and wines in excess of two litres each.
5. Gold or silver, in any form, other than ornaments.

Annex II

1. Colour Television/Monochrome Television.
2. Digital Video Disc Player.
3. Video Home Theatre System.
4. Dish Washer.
5. Music System.
6. Air Conditioner.
7. Domestic refrigerators of capacity above 300 litres or its equivalent.
8. Deep Freezer.
9. Microwave Oven.
10. Video camera or the combination of such video camera with one or more of the following goods, namely :-
    - (a) Television Receiver;
    - (b) Sound recording or reproducing apparatus;
    - (c) Video reproducing apparatus.
11. Word Processing Machine.
12. Fax machine.
13. Portable Photocopying Machine.
14. Vessels.
15. Aircraft.
16. Cinematographic films of 35 mm and above.
17. Gold or silver, in any form, other than ornaments.

Annex III

1. Video Cassette Recorder or Video Cassette Player or Video television receiver or Video Cassette Disc Player.
2. Washing machine.
3. Electrical or LPG Cooking range.
4. Personal Computer (Desk Top).
5. Laptop Computer (Note Book Computer).
6. Domestic Refrigerators of capacity up to 300 litres or its equivalent.

Annex IV

Amritsar:

(1) Amritsar Railway Station

(2) Attari Road

(3) Attari Railway Station

(4) Khalra

Baroda:

(5) Assara Naka

(6) Khavda Naka

(7) Lakhpat

(8) Santalpur Naka

(9) SuigamNaka

Delhi:

(10) Delhi Railway Station

Ferozpur District:

(11) Hussainiwala

Jodhpur Division:

(12) Barmer Railway Station

(13) Munabao Railway Station

Baramullah District:

(14) Adoosa.

4

Regulation & Act of Hotel Classification Standards and Hotel Incentives

TOURISM QUALITY SERVICES AND STANDARDS

Defined and modified by the WTO Quality Support Committee at its sixth meeting (Varadero, Cuba, 9-10 May 2003)

Quality in Tourism

In its work programme WTO is guided by the understanding of quality in tourism as "the result of a process which implies the satisfaction of all the legitimate product and service needs, requirements and expectations of the consumer, at an acceptable price, in conformity with mutually accepted contractual conditions and the underlying quality determinants such as safety and security, hygiene, accessibility, transparency, authenticity and harmony of the tourism activity concerned with its human and natural environment"

The analysis of each term used in this definition suggests concrete actions which can be evaluated from the perspective of quality criteria.

"Result" implies that quality is attained and perceived at a given time. It cannot be in place without harmonious and active engagement of all the factors intervening in tourism experience. The "result" can be measured by consumer satisfaction as well as by social, environmental and economic effects of the tourism activity concerned.

"Process" means that a single undertaking is not sufficient to attain quality. Work towards quality always has to in place, it cannot discontinue because of the temporarily attained quality result. It also implies a seamless or flawless process in which it is possible to identify and do away with the constrains of a supply which spoil the tourism product and are responsible for direct and indirect losses to the company or destination.

"Satisfaction" introduces the elements of subjectivity in quality perception. According to their characteristics, customers have different requirements and expectations. Informed quality-driven marketing caters to these characteristics and attempts to identify consumers according to the different types and levels of perceived quality.

"Legitimate" brings into the analysis the elements of rights and entitlement. Consumers cannot expect to receive more than what they remunerate by payment or what has been determined by social and environmental limits. The role of tourism planners and entrepreneurs is to relate quality types and levels to remuneration and external limitations.

The notion of "needs" follows on the concern for legitimacy and looks for satisfying people's basic and vital needs which should never be overlooked while bringing into tourism projects and programmes the other aspects with a view to introducing attractions, strengthening experiences, etc. The needs are primarily related to the underlying quality determinants, although over time the expectations related to the type and volume of "basic needs" change and usually increase . Basic needs of the past are not exactly the basic needs of today.

The notion of "product requirements" emphasizes a need to relate a single service and facility use to the whole product and the total tourism experience. One good quality service is not sufficient to give rise to tourism product quality perception, although an excellent service may positively impress the consumer to make him or her close their eyes to shortcomings and defects experienced elsewhere in the tourism product.

The term "service requirements" relates quality to its human, personal and personnel dimensions which are often intangible and apparently difficult to measure, evaluate and quantify in contrast with the physical attributes of tourism facilities which are used primarily in facility classifications or grading. However, certain service elements are quantifiable, for example waiting time, frequency of service (e.g. cleaning), the number and type of services included in the basic price, etc.

The term "expectations" relates to the requirement of positive communication and perception of the product characteristics to the potential consumer. There should be no negative surprises at the time of delivery of a service or supply of a product, the consumer must receive what has been promised (or even more). Expectations should also be legitimate, there are limits to expectations, some expectations cannot be fulfilled even at a very high price which can be offered.

The term "consumer" relates to individual (end) consumers, who may include groups of people (e.g. a family), corporate consumers (e.g. a company purchasing an incentive trip) and commercial intermediaries (e.g. a tour operator). The latter may request that the product quality be assessed and certified by its own representative or a recognized external third party.

"Acceptable price" suggests that the client's expectations reflected in the price cannot be attained at any cost, and that "positive surprises" should not be too generous, otherwise this may imply excessive allocation of resources which do not receive adequate remuneration. If quality is guaranteed and the product exceptional, there should be no expectation that it should be sold cheap.

"Mutually accepted contractual conditions" is an additional concept included in the definition by the WTO Quality Support Committee, at the indication of the private sector. It introduces the element of commercial and legal nature and is related to transparency. Acceptance can be explicit or tacit (implicit), depending on the regulations governing the tourism sector in a given country or the type of transaction. For example, some contracts may need to be signed, while other transactions would only require prior communication of the price on ordering a service.

"The underlying quality determinants" suggest that there should be common, irrevocable criteria of quality which are vital for the consumer independently of category or class of the product, establishment, facility or service sophistication. They establish the minimum level of consumer protection under which quality, or total quality, is impossible to achieve, or when failing to meet any of such determinants will significantly reduce the quality of tourism experience.

Safety & Security

A tourism product or service cannot represent danger to life, damage to health and other vital interests and integrity of the consumer (even if we talk about "adventure tourism"). Safety and security standards are normally established by law (e.g. by fire prevention regulations) and should be considered as quality standards per se.

Hygiene

For example, an accommodation facility just has to be safe and clean, one cannot pretend that such requirements are more important to high-class establishments. Food safety standards (often also established by law) must be met and be common to all types of food outlets, from street vendors to luxury gourmet restaurants to airline catering.

Accessibility

This determinant requires that physical, communication and service barriers must be done away with to allow, without discrimination, the use of mainstream tourism products and services by all people irrespective of their natural and acquired differences, including people with disabilities.

"Accessible Tourism for All"

[*Madrid, December 2005*]

"Creating Tourism Opportunities for Handicapped People in the Nineties" [*Madrid, July 1991*]

Conclusions of: The 1st International Congress on "Tourism for All"

[*Islantilla, Spain, 2-4 November 2004*] (For: Arabic, French, Spanish, Russian)

"Cultural and Natural Heritage: Accessibility and Conservation" (For: French, Spanish) and

Presentation by Mr. Henryk Handszuh, Chief, Quality and Trade in Tourism (in Spanish)

International workshop: Tourism for All.

[*Forum Barcelona 2004, Spain, 14 July 2004*]

Transparency

It is a key element to provide for legitimacy of expectations and consumer protection. It relates to providing and effectively communicating truthful information on the characteristics and coverage of the product and its total price. In includes to state what is covered by the price and what is not in the product on supply.

Harmony

Harmony with the human and natural environment pertains to sustainability which is a medium- and long-term concept. "Maintaining the sustainability of tourism requires managing environmental and socio-economic impacts, establishing environmental indicators and maintaining the quality of the tourism products and tourist markets" (WTO Guide for Local Authorities on Developing Sustainable Tourism). There can be no sustainability without quality.

Authenticity

In a commercial world, authenticity is the hardest and most subjective quality determinant to attain. It also has marketing and competition dimensions. Authenticity is culturally determined and one of its results is making the product markedly distinct from other similar products. Authenticity must meet consumer expectations. It diminishes and eventually terminates when the product loses its links with its cultural and natural background. In this sense, a "genuine" ethnic restaurant can never be entirely authentic in a place distinct from its original setting. This does not mean that such an establishment cannot be an attraction and that it cannot be assessed from the viewpoint of quality with respect to production (content and design), marketing, distribution, sale and delivery of the service concerned. A theme park representing other lands and far away cultures is a good example of an initially artificial tourism product which may create an authenticity and a quality image of its own. On the other hand, an authentic product can also develop and adapt to needs and expectations.

WTO POSITION ON TOURISM STANDARDS

(excerpts from the report of the Second Meeting of the Quality Support and Trade Committee, Madrid, 11-12 November 2004)

1. The Committee took note of the increasing role of standards in tourism activities responding to the needs of trade, consumer protection, promotion, marketing, communication and transparency and relating to terminology, management systems and technical specifications. It also took note of the search for international referents in the field and the variety of corresponding national and international activities and initiatives, particularly by the International Organization for Standardization (ISO) aiming to draft such standards.

2. The Committee welcomed the recent initiative undertaken by ISO, on the proposal of its Committee on Consumer Policy (COPOLCO) in which tourism sector organizations were represented, to create a new Technical Committee on tourism standards to deal with tourism terminology and technical specifications, and to develop the already existing quality management standards (ISO 9000/2000; ISO 14000) with a view to adapting them to the specificity of tourism activities.

3. The Committee considered that the already existing ISO standard on tourism terminology should be revised in order to achieve a broader international consensus.

4. With respect to future standards on specifications of services offered by tourism service suppliers, the Committee took note that the principal aim of standardization would be to address primarily the aspects of safety, security, hygiene and accessibility and recommended that the future

standards, whenever touching upon other aspects, provide for the protection of cultural identity and cultural differences.

5. It further recommended that:

- the future ISO Technical Committee on tourism standards provide for a facility to allow representatives of consumer organizations to be permanently involved in the drafting procedure and that the Technical Committee terms of reference would encourage equitable participation from all world regions;
- the first areas for standard development include the activities in which there already exists more substantial national experience.

RAISING QUALITY OF BRITISH TOURISM PRODUCTS

At VisitBritain we are committed to developing the health and vitality of Britain's tourism offer. We want to market only products whose quality is guaranteed to consistently meet and exceed consumers' expectations.

Daily Mail Advertising Opportunity

As part of this drive we are offering Quality assessed accommodation providers the opportunity to advertise with VisitBritain at discounted rates allowing for national exposure.

Integrating Quality and Marketing

VisitBritain with its partners VisitScotland and Wales Tourist Board has responsibility for both assessing the quality of and marketing Britain's tourism products. This integration of quality and promotion creates a unique opportunity to build Britain's long-term position as a quality brand.

Only Quality-Assured

Already all quality-assessed product - irrespective of who it is assessed by - receives prominence in VisitBritain's marketing activities. From 1 January 2006, VisitBritain will market only quality-assured accommodation.

Our aim is to encourage at least 80% of tourism providers to join one of the industry's many quality accreditation schemes by 2010.

Agreement of Common Standards

Say goodbye to the confusion of keys, roses, leeks, thistles, daffodils and frogs. VisitBritain, VisitScotland, Wales Tourist Board, AA and RAC have engineered common standards across all the British accommodation grading systems and are

REGULATIONS ON HOTEL CLASSIFICATION STANDARDS

(Issued in conjunction with the Decision No. 02/2001/ QD-TCDL dated 27 April 2001 of Vietnam National Administration of Tourism).

Hotel is an architectural work built independently with at least 10 rooms upward, meets the quality of physical equipement, appliances and necessary services for touists.

1 to 5 star hotels are the hotels with physical equipement, appliances and high service quality; meet the diversified demand of tourists on board and lodging, daily activities and entertainment in accordance with the standards of each classification which comply with international standards which estimated through criteria:

1. Location and architecture.
2., Facilities and service conveniences.

3. Services and service qualities.
4. Attendant staff.
5. Hygiene.

If hotel is classified with a higher rank, it must have perfect and proficient service quality, physical equipment and the number of services in order to meet the diversified demands of customers.

1. Location and architecture

- Location: Hotels shall be built far from hospital, school at least 100 meters on the basic of the position between the two foundations; not inner or close defense, security areas and protected objections according to present regulations.

Architectural design

— The service line between sections and in each service section of the hotel must be suitable, comfortable and in one way.

— Hotel name board, hotel classification and hotel's badge (if available) shall put in easily seen places (both day and night).

— The hotel's exit and entry are arranged comfortable; must have at least 2 doors, one for guest and one for hotel officials and attendant staff.

— Parking area: Hotel must set up parking lots for guests.

— Room: the minimum surface of bedroom, restroom (m^2):

Bedroom:

— Twins room: 22 m^2.

— Single room: 9 m^2.

— Double room: 14 m^2.

— Room with 3, 4 extra beds: 18 m^2.
— Restroom: 4 m^2.

Hotels for recreational objectives (beach and mountainous resorts...) should have spaces for the 3 extra beds (if required by the guests).

— Lobby: Reception lobby (the space of main entry and exit of the hotel) has to broad enough to welcome visitors in accordance with the hotel scale.
— Restroom at the public areas (reception, dining hall areas...) has ladies and gentlemen room separately.

2. Facilities and service conveniences

Power supply system:

— The illumination meets the demand of each area.
— Ambulance lights in order to take precautions against break - downs.
— Electricity supply availability 24/24 hours for daily activities and services.

Water system:

— Water supply sufficiency to activities and extinguishing a fire 24/24 hours.
— Hot water supply: 24/24 hours.
— Sewage and waste treatment systems must meet the standards of environmental hygiene.
— Extinguish fire equipment: has system of fire alert lights and fire extinguishing gears.
— Public restroom: has been equipped with hand – dryer and napkin.

3. Services and service qualities

Services provided in each hotel are readyly served.

4. Attendant staff

— Professional skills: Managers and attendant staff must be trained and placed in their right professional skills.

— Health: Attendant staff must be medical tested (medical certificate).

— Uniform: Managers and attendant staff have to wear uniform, complication with the hotel regulations for each title and each service section during their working time at the hotel.

5. Hygiene

Hotels have to carry out measures to meet the requirements on hygiene in the following fields:

— Environmental and hotel surroundings' hygiene.

— Hygiene of inside - hotel areas.

— Hygiene of facilities and set of serving tools for guests.

— Food security.

— Personal hygiene (for attendant staff).

THE HOTELS INCENTIVES ACT OF JAMAICA

For the purposes of the Hotels Incentives Act:-

"Hotel" means any building, or group of buildings within the same precinct containing or intended to contain when complete an aggregate number of not less than ten bedrooms and facilities for meals for the accommodation of transient guests, including tourists, for reward, together with the precinct thereof and all other buildings and structures within such precinct.

Under the Hotels Incentives Act, ten years relief from income tax and import duty is available to:-

(a) New hotels

(b) Existing hotels adding a minimum of ten (10) rooms or 30% of the existing number of rooms (whichever is greater).

(c) Existing hotels which have done or intend to do substantial structural alteration.

Approved Convention Hotels with three hundred and fifty (350) or more bedrooms are entitled to income tax and import duty relief ranging from 11-15 years.

Under the Hotels Incentives Act, any company which is recognized as owner, tenant and operator is entitled to benefits.

The applications are processed by the Ministry responsible for Tourism.

Application for Hotel Incentives

Completed Application forms should be forwarded with the following supporting documentation:

— Approved Building Plans
— Copies of Articles and Memorandum of Association, Certificate of Incorporation for Company
— Copy of Certificate of Title to property
— Copy of letters of confirmation from funding sources
— Copy of management/lease agreement (if operator of property is different from owner)

RESORT COTTAGES INCENTIVES ACT

For the purposes of the Resort Cottages Incentives Act:-

"Resort Cottages" means any building containing or intended to contain when completed not less than two furnished bedrooms, a furnished living room, bathroom facilities and facilities for the preparation of meals, and used or intended to be used for the accommodation of transient guests including tourists for reward.

"Group of Resort Cottages" means two or more cottages

a. containing an aggregate number of not less than 10 bedrooms;

b. situated in the same district village or town; and

c. owned by the same person.

New Resort Cottages are entitled to 7 years relief from income tax.

Groups of Resort Cottages are entitled to 7years relief from importation duties.

Under the Resort Cottages Act, owners, tenants or operators of resort cottages or groups of resort cottages are entitled to benefits.

Applications are processed by the Ministry with responsibility for Tourism.

Re: Application for Resort Cottage Incentives

Completed Application forms, signed and dated, must be returned with the following supporting documentation:

1. Approved Building Plans
2. Copies of Articles and Memorandum of Association, Certificate of Incorporation for Company
3. Copy of Certificate of Title to property
4. Copy of letters of confirmation from funding sources
5. Copy of management/lease agreement (if operator of property is different from owner).

SHORT TERM INCENTIVE PACKAGE(STIP) II OF ASSISTANCE TO THE TOURISM INDUSTRY

Background

1. The Ministry of Tourism & Sport requested approval from Cabinet for a second round of the Short-Term Incentive Package (STIP) of Assistance to the Tourism Industry when it was determined that the first incentive package was significantly under-subscribed. On October 1, 2001, Cabinet approved the request.

What is Covered

2. Cabinet has approved the following for the Short-Term Incentive Package (STIP) II:

(a) granting of General Consumption Tax and customs duty benefits on specific items bought locally or imported for the refurbishment and/or expansion of accommodation facilities (particularly small and medium sized properties) that do not currently qualify to receive benefits under existing incentive legislation, i.e. HIA and RCIA

(b) that in the case of large properties of over 100 rooms, a rigorous assessment will be undertaken to determine their eligibility for benefits under the Short Term Incentive Programme (STIP) II.

Mechanisms for Access

3. Applications under the scheme must be made within an eighteen (18) month period after the date of approval by Cabinet.

4. All benefits to be derived can be accessed within a maximum of two (2) years after the date of approval of individual applications.

5. A Committee to review applications has been

established by the Minister of Tourism and Sport and will meet twice per month or as the need arises. It is comprised of representatives from the following:

- — Ministry of Tourism & Sport (Chair)
- — Tourism Product Development Company (TPDCo)
- — Jamaica Tourist Board (JTB)
- — Jamaica Hotel and Tourist Association (JHTA)
- — Association of Jamaica Attractions Limited (AJAL
- — Jamaica Association of Villas and Apartments (JAVA)
- — Ministry of Commerce and Technology (MCT)
- — Ministry of Finance and Planning
- — Jamaica Customs
- — Taxpayers Audit & Assessment Department (TAAD)

Where to get Applications

Applications are available at:

- — Ministry Of Tourism and Sport 3rd floor, 64 Knutsford Boulevard Kingston 5. Tel: 920-4926-30 Fax: 920-4944
- — JAMAICA Hotel and Tourist Association 2 Ardenne Road Kingston 10. Tel: 926-3635/6 Fax: 929-1054
- — Tourism Product Development Company 4th floor, 64 Knutsford Boulevard Kingston 5. Tel: 968-3441, 968-3626, 968-8893-4Fax: 929-8269(TPDCo offices also located in Ocho Rios & Montego Bay)
- — JAMAICA Association Of Villas and Apartments Pineapple Place P.O. Box 298 Ocho Rios P.O., St. Ann Tel: 974-2508, 974-2763 Fax: 973-2967
- — THE JAMAICA Tourist Board 64 Knutsford Boulevard Kingston 5. Tel: 929-9200-9 Fax: 929-9375(JTB offices also located in Negril, Montego Bay, Ocho Rios, Port Antonio, & Black River)

— Association Of Jamaican Attractions Limited 66 Claude Clarke Avenue, Montego Bay, St. James Tel: 952-0889 Fax: 979-7437

Short Term Incentive Package (STIP) II

Supporting Documents Required

— The Application form should be accompanied by a non-refundable processing fee of 0.01% of the total investment cost of the project, or, $2,500.00 whichever is greater. Only manager's cheques will be accepted and these should be made payable to the Tourism Product Development Co. Ltd.

— Completed applications should be forwarded to the Jamaica Hotel & Tourist Association (JHTA), the Jamaica Association of Villas and Apartments (JAVA) and to the Association of Jamaica Attractions Limited (AJAL) [for members of the respective associations]. Accommodations and attractions that are not members of the named associations should forward applications directly to the Ministry of Tourism & Sport, 3rd Floor Jamaica Tourism Centre, 64 Knutsford Boulevard, Kingston 5; Attention Short Term Incentives Package II.

The Following Supporting Documentation is Required in Order for the Application to be Processed:

1. Copies of Certificate of Incorporation, Memorandum and Articles of Association (if a company makes application). A Certificate of Registration of Business Name is required for sole traders.
2. Copy of Certificate of Title / Lease or Management Agreement
3. List of items and quantities to be purchased certified by TPDCo (for those entities undertaking

refurbishing that does not involve any construction e.g. re-furnishing and/or re-equipping).

4. Pro-forma invoice(s)
5. Copy of Tax Compliance Certificate.
6. Certified Copy of Balance Sheet for last year of operation.
7. Copy of JTB License/TPDCo Inspection Report
8. Photograph of facility (8" x 10")/Brochure

For those facilities undergoing major refurbishing or upgrading a Quantity Surveyor's Report and a copy of the approved Building Plan/Drawing designating the precinct of the existing structure and the proposed extension is also required. (Additional charges will apply where necessary).

For new businesses/entities, a business plan is also required.

Incentives for Tourist Attractions Under the Short Term Incentive Programme

Definition of Tourist Attraction

Tourist Attraction is a natural or man-made entity, which offers horticultural, cultural, historical, equestrian, aquatic or aerial activities for reward or profit.

Natural Attraction: Focuses on environment or natural areas of a Country, e.g. National Parks, Nature Reserves, Botanical Gardens, Marina Parks.

Heritage Attractions: Relates to history of the country e.g. colonial building, indigenous sites, archaeological sites.

Man made Attractions: Such as theme parks, seaquariums as approved by the committee.

Cultural Attractions: A permanent site for cultural attraction, music and drama festivals.

Within the above context, a site can be considered an attraction if one or more of the following conditions apply:

— It has an established monitoring system, which includes, but is not restricted to, a mechanism for measuring the number of visitors it receives.

— It is managed by either a government body, private sector or by an NGO

— It charges an admission fee

5

Global Codes of Ethics for Tourism

Principles

The Code includes nine Article s outlining the "rules of the game" for destinations, governments, tour operators, developers, travel agents, workers and travellers themselves. The tenth Article involves the redress of grievances and marks the first time that a code of this type will have a mechanism for enforcement.

Article 1

Tourism's contribution to mutual understanding and respect between peoples and societies

Article 2

Tourism as a vehicle for individual and collective fulfilment

Article 3

Tourism, a factor of sustainable development

Article 4

Tourism, a user of the cultural heritage of mankind and contributor to its enhancement

Article 5

Tourism, a beneficial activity for host countries and communities

Article 6

Obligations of stakeholders in tourism development

Article 7

Right to tourism

Article 8

Liberty of tourist movements

Article 9

Rights of the workers and entrepreneurs in the tourism industry

Article 10

Implementation of the principles of the Global Code of Ethics for Tourism

Article 1

Tourism's Contribution to Mutual Understanding and Respect between Peoples and Societies

The understanding and promotion of the ethical values common to humanity, with an attitude of tolerance and respect for the diversity of religious, philosophical and moral beliefs, are both the foundation and the consequence of responsible tourism; stakeholders in tourism development and tourists themselves should observe the social and cultural traditions and practices of all peoples, including those of minorities and indigenous peoples and to recognize their worth;

Tourism activities should be conducted in harmony with the attributes and traditions of the host regions and countries and in respect for their laws, practices and customs;

The host communities, on the one hand, and local professionals, on the other, should acquaint themselves with and respect the tourists who visit them and find out about their lifestyles, tastes and expectations; the education and training imparted to professionals contribute to a hospitable welcome;

It is the task of the public authorities to provide protection for tourists and visitors and their belongings; they must pay particular attention to the safety of foreign tourists owing to the particular vulnerability they may have; they should facilitate the introduction of specific means of information, prevention, security, insurance and assistance consistent with their needs; any attacks, assaults, kidnappings or threats against tourists or workers in the tourism industry, as well as the wilful destruction of tourism facilities or of elements of cultural or natural heritage should be severely condemned and punished in accordance with their respective national laws;

When travelling, tourists and visitors should not commit any criminal act or any act considered criminal by the laws of the country visited and abstain from any conduct felt to be offensive or injurious by the local populations, or likely to damage the local environment; they should refrain from all trafficking in illicit drugs, arms, antiques, protected species and products and substances that are dangerous or prohibited by national regulations;

Tourists and visitors have the responsibility to acquaint themselves, even before their departure, with the characteristics of the countries they are preparing to visit; they must be aware of the health and security risks inherent in any travel outside their usual environment and behave in such a way as to minimize those risks.

Article 2

Tourism as a Vehicle for Individual and Collective Fulfilment

Tourism, the activity most frequently associated with rest and relaxation, sport and access to culture and nature, should be planned and practised as a privileged means of individual and collective fulfilment; when practised with a sufficiently open mind, it is an irreplaceable factor of self-education, mutual tolerance and for learning about the legitimate differences between peoples and cultures and their diversity;

Tourism activities should respect the equality of men and women; they should promote human rights and, more particularly, the individual rights of the most vulnerable groups, notably children, the elderly, the handicapped, ethnic minorities and indigenous peoples;

The exploitation of human beings in any form, particularly sexual, especially when applied to children, conflicts with the fundamental aims of tourism and is the negation of tourism; as such, in accordance with international law, it should be energetically combatted with the cooperation of all the States concerned and penalized without concession by the national legislation of both the countries visited and the countries of the perpetrators of these acts, even when they are carried out abroad;

Travel for purposes of religion, health, education and cultural or linguistic exchanges are particularly beneficial forms of tourism, which deserve encouragement;

The introduction into curricula of education about the value of tourist exchanges, their economic, social and cultural benefits, and also their risks, should be encouraged;

Article 3

Tourism, a Factor of Sustainable Development

All the stakeholders in tourism development should safeguard the natural environment with a view to achieving sound, continuous and sustainable economic growth geared to satisfying equitably the needs and aspirations of present and future generations;

All forms of tourism development that are conducive to saving rare and precious resources, in particular water and energy, as well as avoiding so far as possible waste production, should be given priority and encouraged by national, regional and local public authorities;

The staggering in time and space of tourist and visitor flows, particularly those resulting from paid leave and school holidays, and a more even distribution of holidays should be sought so as to reduce the pressure of tourism activity on the environment and enhance its beneficial impact on the tourism industry and the local economy;

Tourism infrastructure should be designed and tourism activities programmed in such a way as to protect the natural heritage composed of ecosystems and biodiversity and to preserve endangered species of wildlife; the stakeholders in tourism development, and especially professionals, should agree to the imposition of limitations or constraints on their activities when these are exercised in particularly sensitive areas: desert, polar or high mountain regions, coastal areas, tropical forests or wetlands, propitious to the creation of nature reserves or protected areas;

Nature tourism and ecotourism are recognized as being particularly conducive to enriching and enhancing the standing of tourism, provided they respect the natural heritage and local populations and are in keeping with the carrying capacity of the sites;

Article 4

Tourism, a User of the Cultural Heritage of Mankind and Contributor to its Enhancement

Tourism resources belong to the common heritage of mankind; the communities in whose territories they are situated have particular rights and obligations to them;

Tourism policies and activities should be conducted with respect for the artistic, archaeological and cultural heritage, which they should protect and pass on to future generations; particular care should be devoted to preserving and upgrading monuments, shrines and museums as well as archaeological and historic sites which must be widely open to tourist visits; encouragement should be given to public access to privately-owned cultural property and monuments, with respect for the rights of their owners, as well as to religious buildings, without prejudice to normal needs of worship;

Financial resources derived from visits to cultural sites and monuments should, at least in part, be used for the upkeep, safeguard, development and embellishment of this heritage;

Tourism activity should be planned in such a way as to allow traditional cultural products, crafts and folklore to survive and flourish, rather than causing them to degenerate and become standardized;

Article 5

Tourism, a Beneficial Activity for Host Countries and Communities

Local populations should be associated with tourism activities and share equitably in the economic, social and cultural benefits they generate, and particularly in the creation of direct and indirect jobs resulting from them;

Tourism policies should be applied in such a way as to help to raise the standard of living of the populations of the regions visited and meet their needs; the planning and architectural approach to and operation of tourism resorts and accommodation should aim to integrate them, to the extent possible, in the local economic and social fabric; where skills are equal, priority should be given to local manpower;

Special attention should be paid to the specific problems of coastal areas and island territories and to vulnerable rural or mountain regions, for which tourism often represents a rare opportunity for development in the face of the decline of traditional economic activities;

Tourism professionals, particularly investors, governed by the regulations laid down by the public authorities, should carry out studies of the impact of their development projects on the environment and natural surroundings; they should also deliver, with the greatest transparency and objectivity, information on their future programmes and their foreseeable repercussions and foster dialogue on their contents with the populations concerned;

Article 6

Obligations of Stakeholders in Tourism Development

Tourism professionals have an obligation to provide tourists with objective and honest information on their places of destination and on the conditions of travel, hospitality and stays; they should ensure that the contractual clauses proposed to their customers are readily understandable as to the nature, price and quality of the services they commit themselves to providing and the financial compensation payable by them in the event of a unilateral breach of contract on their part;

Tourism professionals, insofar as it depends on them, should show concern, in co-operation with the public authorities, for the security and safety, accident prevention, health protection and food safety of those who seek their services; likewise, they should ensure the existence of suitable systems of insurance and assistance; they should accept the reporting obligations prescribed by national regulations and pay fair compensation in the event of failure to observe their contractual obligations;

Tourism professionals, so far as this depends on them, should contribute to the cultural and spiritual fulfilment of tourists and allow them, during their travels, to practise their religions;

The public authorities of the generating States and the host countries, in cooperation with the professionals concerned and their associations, should ensure that the necessary mechanisms are in place for the repatriation of tourists in the event of the bankruptcy of the enterprise that organized their travel;

Governments have the right – and the duty - especially in a crisis, to inform their nationals of the difficult circumstances, or even the dangers they may encounter during their travels abroad; it is their responsibility however to issue such information without prejudicing in an unjustified or exaggerated manner the tourism industry of the host countries and the interests of their own operators; the contents of travel advisories should therefore be discussed beforehand with the authorities of the host countries and the professionals concerned; recommendations formulated should be strictly proportionate to the gravity of the situations encountered and confined to the geographical areas where the insecurity has arisen; such advisories should be qualified or cancelled as soon as a return to normality permits;

The press, and particularly the specialized travel press and the other media, including modern means of electronic communication, should issue honest and balanced information on events and situations that could influence the flow of tourists; they should also provide accurate and reliable information to the consumers of tourism services; the new communication and electronic commerce technologies should also be developed and used for this purpose; as is the case for the media, they should not in any way promote sex tourism;

Article 7

Right to Tourism

The prospect of direct and personal access to the discovery

and enjoyment of the planet's resources constitutes a right equally open to all the world's inhabitants; the increasingly extensive participation in national and international tourism should be regarded as one of the best possible expressions of the sustained growth of free time, and obstacles should not be placed in its way;

The universal right to tourism must be regarded as the corollary of the right to rest and leisure, including reasonable limitation of working hours and periodic holidays with pay, guaranteed by Article 24 of the Universal Declaration of Human Rights and Article 7.d of the International Covenant on Economic, Social and Cultural Rights; Social tourism, and in particular associative tourism, which facilitates widespread access to leisure, travel and holidays, should be developed with the support of the public authorities;

Family, youth, student and senior tourism and tourism for people with disabilities, should be encouraged and facilitated;

Article 8

Liberty of Tourist Movements

Tourists and visitors should benefit, in compliance with international law and national legislation, from the liberty to move within their countries and from one State to another, in accordance with Article 13 of the Universal Declaration of Human Rights; they should have access to places of transit and stay and to tourism and cultural sites without being subject to excessive formalities or discrimination;

Tourists and visitors should have access to all available forms of communication, internal or external; they should benefit from prompt and easy access to local administrative, legal and health services; they should be free to contact the consular representatives of their countries of origin in compliance with the diplomatic conventions in force;

Tourists and visitors should benefit from the same rights as the citizens of the country visited concerning the confidentiality of the personal data and information concerning them, especially when these are stored electronically;

Administrative procedures relating to border crossings whether they fall within the competence of States or result from international agreements, such as visas or health and customs formalities, should be adapted, so far as possible, so as to facilitate to the maximum freedom of travel and widespread access to international tourism; agreements between groups of countries to harmonize and simplify these procedures should be encouraged; specific taxes and levies penalizing the tourism industry and undermining its competitiveness should be gradually phased out or corrected;

So far as the economic situation of the countries from which they come permits, travellers should have access to allowances of convertible currencies needed for their travels;

Article 9

Rights of the Workers and Entrepreneurs in the Tourism Industry

The fundamental rights of salaried and self-employed workers in the tourism industry and related activities, should be guaranteed under the supervision of the national and local administrations, both of their States of origin and of the host countries with particular care, given the specific constraints linked in particular to the seasonality of their activity, the global dimension of their industry and the flexibility often required of them by the nature of their work;

Salaried and self-employed workers in the tourism industry and related activities have the right and the duty to acquire appropriate initial and continuous training; they should be given adequate social protection; job insecurity should be limited so far as possible; and a specific status, with particular regard to their social welfare, should be offered to seasonal workers in the sector;

Any natural or legal person, provided he, she or it has the necessary abilities and skills, should be entitled to develop a professional activity in the field of tourism under existing national laws; entrepreneurs and investors - especially in the area of small and medium-sized enterprises - should be entitled to free access to the tourism sector with a minimum of legal or administrative restrictions;

Exchanges of experience offered to executives and workers, whether salaried or not, from different countries, contributes to foster the development of the world tourism industry; these movements should be facilitated so far as possible in compliance with the applicable national laws and international conventions;

As an irreplaceable factor of solidarity in the development and dynamic growth of international exchanges, multinational enterprises of the tourism industry should not exploit the dominant positions they sometimes occupy; they should avoid becoming the vehicles of cultural and social models artificially imposed on the host communities; in exchange for their freedom to invest and trade which should be fully recognized, they should involve themselves in local development, avoiding, by the excessive repatriation of their profits or their induced imports, a reduction of their contribution to the economies in which they are established;

Partnership and the establishment of balanced relations between enterprises of generating and receiving countries contribute to the sustainable development of tourism and an equitable distribution of the benefits of its growth;

Article 10

Implementation of the Principles of the Global Code of Ethics for Tourism

The public and private stakeholders in tourism development should cooperate in the implementation of these principles and monitor their effective application;

The stakeholders in tourism development should recognize the role of international institutions, among which the World Tourism Organization ranks first, and non-governmental organizations with competence in the field of tourism promotion and development, the protection of human rights, the environment or health, with due respect for the general principles of international law;

The same stakeholders should demonstrate their intention to refer any disputes concerning the application or interpretation of the Global Code of Ethics for Tourism for conciliation to an impartial third body known as the World Committee on Tourism Ethics.

Annexure

PROTOCOL OF IMPLEMENTATION

Body responsible for interpreting, applying and evaluating the provisions of the Global Code of Ethics for Tourism

(a) A World Committee on Tourism Ethics shall be created comprising twelve eminent persons independent of governments and twelve alternates, selected on the basis of their competence in the field of tourism and related fields; they shall not receive any orders or instructions from those who proposed their nomination or who designated them and shall not report to them;

(b) The members of the World Committee on Tourism Ethics shall be appointed as follows:

- six members and six alternate members designated by the WTO Regional Commissions, on the proposal of the States Members of WTO;
- a member and an alternate designated by the autonomous territories that are Associate Members of WTO from among their members;
- four members and four alternate members elected by the WTO General Assembly from among the Affiliate Members of WTO representing professionals or employees of the tourism industry, universities and non-governmental organizations, after conferring with the Committee of Affiliate Members;
- a chairman, who may be an eminent person not belonging to WTO, elected by the other members of the Committee, on the proposal of the Secretary-General of WTO;

The Legal Adviser of the World Tourism Organization shall participate, when necessary, and in an advisory capacity, in the Committee meetings; the Secretary-General shall attend ex officio or may arrange to be represented at its meetings;

On appointing the members of the Committee, account shall be taken of the need for a balanced geographical composition of this body and for a diversification of the qualifications and personal status of its members, from both the economic and social as well as the legal viewpoint; the members shall be appointed for four years and their term of office may be renewed only once; in the event of a vacancy, the member shall be replaced by his alternate, it being understood that if the vacancy concerns both the member and his alternate, the Committee itself shall fill the vacant seat; if the

Chairman's seat is vacant he or she shall be replaced in the conditions set out above;

(c) The WTO Regional Commissions shall act, in the cases provided for in paragraphs I(d), (g) and (h), as well as II(a), (b), (f) and (g) below of this Protocol, as regional committees on tourism ethics;

(d) The World Committee on Tourism Ethics shall establish its own Rules of Procedure, which shall apply equally, mutatis mutandis, to the Regional Commissions when these are acting as regional committees on tourism ethics; the presence of two-thirds of the Committee members shall be necessary to constitute a quorum at its meetings; in the event that a member is absent, he may be replaced by his alternate; in the event of a tie in the voting, the chairman shall have the casting vote;

(e) When proposing the candidature of an eminent person to serve on the Committee, each Member of WTO shall undertake to cover the travel expenses and daily subsistence allowances occasioned by the participation in the meetings of the person whose nomination it has proposed, it being understood that the members of the Committee shall not receive any remuneration; the expenses incurred by the participation of the Chairman of the Committee, also unremunerated, may be borne by the WTO budget; the secretariat of the Committee shall be provided by the services of WTO; the operating costs remaining payable by the Organization may, wholly or in part, be charged to a trust fund financed by voluntary contributions;

(f) The World Committee on Tourism Ethics shall meet in principle once a year; whenever a dispute is referred to it for settlement, the chairman shall consult the other members and the Secretary-General of WTO about the expediency of convening an extraordinary meeting;

(g) The functions of the World Committee on Tourism Ethics and the WTO Regional Commissions shall be the evaluation of the implementation of this Code and conciliation; it may invite experts or external institutions to contribute to its proceedings;

(h) On the basis of periodic reports submitted to them by Full Members, Associate Members and Affiliate Members of WTO, the WTO Regional Commissions shall, every two years, as regional committees on tourism ethics, examine the application of the Code in their respective regions; they shall record their findings in a report to the World Committee on Tourism Ethics; the reports of the Regional Commissions may contain suggestions to amend or supplement the Global Code of Ethics for Tourism;

(i) The World Committee on Tourism Ethics shall exercise a global function as a "watchdog" for the problems encountered in implementing the Code and for the proposed solutions; it shall summarize the reports drawn up by the Regional Commissions and supplement them with the information it has collected with the assistance of the Secretary-General and the support of the Committee of Affiliate Members, which shall include, should the need arise, proposals to amend or supplement the Global Code of Ethics for Tourism;

(j) The Secretary-General shall refer the report of the World Committee on Tourism Ethics to the Executive Council, together with his own observations, for consideration and transmission to the General Assembly with the Council's recommendations;

the General Assembly shall decide what follow-up action to take on the report and the recommendations thus submitted to it, which the national tourism administrations and other stakeholders in the tourism development shall subsequently have the task of implementing;

Conciliation Mechanism for the Settlement of Disputes

(a) In the event of a dispute concerning the interpretation or application of the Global Code of Ethics for Tourism, two or more stakeholders in tourism development may jointly refer it to the World Committee on Tourism Ethics; if the dispute is between two or more stakeholders belonging to the same region, the Parties should refer the matter to the competent WTO Regional Commission in its capacity as a regional committee on tourism ethics;

(b) The States, as well as tourism enterprises and bodies, may declare that they accept in advance the competence of the World Committee on Tourism Ethics or of a WTO Regional Commission for any dispute concerning the interpretation or application of this Code, or for certain categories of dispute; in this case, the Committee or the competent Regional Commission shall be considered as validly referred to unilaterally by the other Party to the dispute;

(c) When a dispute is submitted in the first instance to the World Committee on Tourism Ethics for consideration, its chairman shall appoint a sub-committee of three members who shall be responsible for examining the dispute;

(d) The World Committee on Tourism Ethics to which a dispute has been referred shall reach a decision on the basis of the record drawn up by the Parties to the dispute; the Committee may ask these Parties for additional information and, if deemed useful, may hear them at their request; the expenses incurred by this hearing shall be borne by the Parties unless the circumstances are considered exceptional by the Committee; the failure of one of the Parties to appear even though he or she has been given a reasonable opportunity to participate, shall not prevent the Committee from making a ruling;

(e) Unless otherwise agreed by the Parties, the World Committee on Tourism Ethics shall announce its decision within three months of the date on which it was referred to; it shall present recommendations to the Parties suitable to form the basis of a settlement; the Parties shall immediately inform the chairman of the Committee that has examined the dispute of the action they have taken on these recommendations;

(f) If a dispute is referred to a WTO Regional Commission, it shall announce its decision following the same procedure, mutatis mutandis, as that applied by the World Committee on Tourism Ethics when it intervenes in the first instance;

(g) If within a period of two months after notification of the proposals of the Committee or of a Regional Commission the Parties have failed to agree on the terms of a final settlement, the Parties or one of them may refer the dispute to a plenary session of the World Committee on Tourism Ethics; when the Committee has made a ruling in the first instance, the members that served on the sub-committee that examined the dispute may not take part in this plenary session and shall be replaced by their alternates; if these intervened in the first instance, the members shall not be prevented from participating;

(h) The plenary session of the World Committee on Tourism Ethics shall make its ruling following the procedure laid out in paragraphs II(d) and (e) above; if no solution has been found at a previous stage, it shall formulate final conclusions for the settlement of the dispute, which the Parties, if they agree with their contents, will be recommended to apply at the earliest possible opportunity; these conclusions shall be made public, even if the process of conciliation has not been successfully completed and one of the Parties refuses to accept the final conclusions proposed;

(i) Full Members, Associate Members and Affiliate Members of WTO, as well as States that are not members of WTO, may declare that they accept in advance as binding and, where applicable, subject to the sole reservation of reciprocity, the final conclusions of the World Committee on Tourism Ethics in the disputes, or in a private dispute to which they are party;

(j) Likewise, the States may accept as binding or subject to exequatur the final conclusions of the World Committee on Tourism Ethics in disputes to which their nationals are party or which should be applied in their territory;

(k) Tourism enterprises and bodies may include in their contractual documents a provision making the final conclusions of the World Committee on Tourism Ethics binding in their relations with their contracting parties.

6

Tourism Codes of Conduct and Codes of Ethics

CODE OF ETHICS: GHAY AND LESBIAN TOURISM AUSTRALIA (GALTA)

These are principals of professional conduct and are to be followed by all GALTA members. Members should have appropriate policies in place, with all directors and employees trained in and instructed to adhere to the following policies:

1. An anti-discrimination and equal opportunity employment policy.
2. Recognition of defacto relationships in all employment benefits including superannuation.
3. Be prepared to be publicly visible in seeking business from the lesbian and gay community.
4. Be prepared to identify themselves as a member of GALTA, in advertising, sponsor-ship and general marketing to the lesbian and gay community.
5. Maintain the highest standards of principles in the conduct of business with other GALTA members and the lesbian and gay community.

This will include the following:

Accuracy. Factual and accurate information, without misleading or doubtful superlatives in advertising or any deceptive practice.

Compliance. With all Australian Federal and State laws and regulations including appropriate business and tour insureances and use of safe (trust) accounts for all deposits as legally required.

Conflict of Interest. Members will not allow any preferred relationship with a supplier to interfere with the interests of the client.

Disclosure. Provide complete details in writing to the client concerning terms and conditions of any service and charges including cancellation policy before accepting a non refundable deposit or payment.

Responsiveness. To be prompt and courteous with all client concerns and possible source of complaint including early advise of cancellation or of any changes in itinerary, services, features or prices.

Co-operation. With any enquiry conducted by GALTA or its representative to resolve a dispute.

6. Follow the GALTA accreditation system of a minimum standard for lesbian and gay accommodation providers, including payment of commissions by accommodation providers to fellow GALTA members as arranged in writing or as shown in any other, or GALTA publication.
7. Eliminate any practice, which could be damaging to other service providers that you represent or to the lesbian and gay tourism industry or its consumers.

8. Take immediate steps to amicably deal with any complaint from a fellow member or where it may be helpful, refer the matter to the GALTA Ethics Committee for that committee to arrange mediation.
9. When requested, provide fair objective and impartial representation of other GALTA service providers avoiding controversy.
10. Minimise environmental impact of tourism by offering information, leading by example and encouraging corrective action to prevent damage.
11. The GALTA name and logo may not be used:
    (a) On legal documents.
    (b) In explicit sexual advertising, for sexual accessories or for tourism activities which involve sexual exploitation.
    (c) By non-members. (Usage must be withdrawn immediately on expiry of GALTA membership.)
12. Encourage and promote membership of GALTA. Membership will assist lesbian and gay consumers and your staff to benefit from training, market experience, information, education and networking events and the many other facilities a strong, active and large membership base will be able to provide.

If a member fails to attend to any one of these ethical standards, the GALTA Ethics Committee may suspend membership rights of that member and or ask the member to resign. If non-compliance continues the matter will be dealt with according to the Gay And Lesbian Tourism Australia Ltd. (GALTA) Constitution and rules.

TASK FORCE TO PROTECT CHILDRENFROM SEXUAL EXPLOITATION IN TOURISM

(London, 14 November 2005)

1. The Task Force to Protect Children from Sexual Exploitation in Tourism held its seventeenth meeting in London on 14 November 2005, as part of parallel events held during the World Travel Market (WTM 2005). The meeting, which was attended by over 60 delegates, featured a Special Session on Government Actions to Combat the Sexual Exploitation of Children in Tourism (SECT).

Opening Remarks

2. The Chairman of the Executive Committee of the Task Force, UNWTO Deputy Secretary-General Dr. Dawid de Villiers, opened the Task Force meeting by welcoming participants from twenty governments, five intergovernmental organizations, eight international or regional industry associations, seven national associations and companies, ten non-governmental organizations (NGOs) and four education institutions.

3. The Chairman mentioned the growing awareness of the Task Force as an open forumto exchange ideas and provide information on activities carried out to prevent and fight against SECT. He underlined the remarkable progress in the strengthening of this network since its establishment in 1997, notably in the number of participants attending the two regular annual meetings and in the countries that had developed initiatives to address the problem.

4. Moreover, Dr. de Villiers presented the major findings of the UNWTO Survey on the Implementation of the Global Code of Ethics for Tourism based on the information collected from Member States and Affiliate Members. He mentioned that nearly three-quarters ofrespondents had already

incorporated the principles of the Code into their legislative texts or had used them as a basis when establishing national laws, regulations or tourism development plans. He also pointed out that the Code had been widely disseminated to tourismstakeholders and also translated by 35 countries into their respective national or local languages. As an example of its international recognition, he made reference to the Geotourism Charter established by National Geographic which adhered to the principles embodied in the Global Code of Ethics.

5. Finally, the Chairman presented a simplified version of the Global Code of Ethics for Tourism entitled The Responsible Tourist and Traveller drafted by the Task Force and adopted by the World Committee on Tourism Ethics at its last meeting held in Tunis on May 2005. The aim of this new document was to make tourists aware of the principles stated in the Code of Ethics, in an user-friendly manner. Dr. de Villiers also mentioned that it would be published as an attractive leaflet and distributed to the travelling public through travel agencies, accommodation establishments and others.

Special Session

Government Actions to Combat the Sexual Exploitation of Children in Tourism

6. Mr. Sidney Alves Costa, Head of Cabinet of the Ministry of Tourism of Brazil, presented the "Sustainable Tourism and Childhood" programme whose main objective was to exchange previous experiences and best practices on protecting children from sexual exploitation in tourism (SECT). The celebration of a seminar on this topic in the framework of the First World Tourism Forum for Peace and Sustainable Development in 2004 was one of the first steps. Other major outcomes were the implementation of an Action Plan and the development of a National Campaign called "Brazil. Love and protect it", promoting a positive

approach in key aspects such as the respect of national diversity, gender and sex issues, ethnic background and relationship between children and tourists. Mr. Alves Costa said that the respect of children's rights was one of the main concerns of governments in the Americas, and that the Brazilian Ministry of Tourism held in 2005 the First Meeting of Ministers and High Authorities in Tourism of South America on the Prevention of SECT. At this meeting, participants agreed to establish a Regional Action Plan to promote cooperation in this field, as well as to create a regional Task Force to protect children following the example of the UNWTO International Task Force. Presentation of Mr. Alves Costa.

7. Ms. Petra Cruz, Director for Europe of the State Secretariat for Tourism of theDominican Republic, presented her country's Campaign and National Plan of Action which included the design of an advertising campaign and the creation of an Inter-institutional Commission against the Commercial and Sexual Abuse and Exploitation of Minors. The aimof this Commission is to propose, coordinate and promote measures against SECT that involve various tourism stakeholders and governmental bodies. She further gave an outline of the training programmes -based on the UNWTO Tourism Training Modules- which are addressed to tourism professionals and to staff of Dominican consulates and tourist boards in Europe. Some of the actions undertaken (viz. the publication of brochures and posters in different languages, and the distribution of tourist cards with warnings about the legal consequences of sexually exploiting minors) received technical and financial support from UNICEF, the Italian Foreign Ministry and the UNICEF German Committee. Finally, Ms. Cruz explained that the ads on TV and cinema as well as other training activities were supported at national level by the International Labour Organization and the Department of Labour of the United States. Presentation of Ms. Cruz.

8. Ms. Diana Tamashiro, Domestic Tourism Manager of the Promotion Board of Peru (PROMPERU) reported on the National Campaign on Prevention of Commercial Sexual Exploitation of Children and Youth in Tourism carried out by the Ministry of Foreign Trade and Tourism. This project was supported by the Lombardia Region of Italy through the NGO CESVI, and by UNICEF which provided technical and financial assistance. She mentioned the training workshops held in Cusco, Trujillo and Iquitos aimed at local tourism students, hotel staff, travel agencies, guides, taxi and "mototaxi" drivers. A guide for suppliers of tourism services, "From Spectators to Actors", and a trainer's guide were also published. The major actions of the campaign involved sensitising travellers through in-flight videos and disseminating brochures and posters to be displayed at airports and by travel agencies. Ms. Tamashiro also mentioned a regional initiative in Iquitos informing tourists, through ads, that the sexual exploitation of children is punishable by law. Presentation of Ms. Tamashiro

9. Mr. Prathap Ramanujam, Permanent Secretary of the Ministry of Tourism of Sri Lanka, presented a project, supported by UNICEF, aimed at increasing community awareness in areas affected by Child Sex Tourism (CST), by means of ensuring that all tourists were aware of the tourism industry's zero tolerance in this field. He reminded that it was also necessary to involve the private sector to play a proactive role and to bring in new policies, laws and regulations to combat this problem. Mr. Ramanujam mentioned that many District Child Protection Councils had been set up in tourist areas in order to improve the coordination and efforts with the police, social authorities, NGOs and other tourismstakeholders. He also reported on some actions that were being implemented, such as the preparation of modules on child rights to be made available to school students and the general public, also in Sinhala and Tamil language; the publishing of catalogues, brochures

and advertisements against CST in different languages; and the development of an in-flight video and website. Finally, Mr. Ramanujam underlined that the Sri Lanka Tourist Board was committed to eradicate Child Sex Tourism in his country so that their children could live free from sexual abuse and exploitation. Full report of Mr. Ramanujam

10.Ms. Anita Dodds, Tourism Programme Manager of Child Wise Australia, presented the ASEAN Regional Public Education Campaign which, with the support of the Australian Government, was being carried out jointly between the ten ASEAN Governments under the coordination of Child Wise Australia. She reminded that there had been 50 million visitor arrivals to the ASEAN region in 2004 representing the highest number of visitors on record, and that increasing tourism in these countries had always been matched with prevention and protection measures for children. Ms. Dodds also mentioned that the Australian Government action involved a wide range of ministries including Aus AID -Agency for International Development-, Ministry of Justice and Customs and the Department of Foreign Affairs and Trade. In this regard, she said, the AusAID had provided financial assistance to Child Wise to facilitate the Campaign, whose objectives were:

(a) to mobilize responsible travellers and local citizens to report suspicious behavior;
(b) to deter child sex offenders, and
(c) to create a culture of intolerance to child sexual abuse.

Ms. Dodds recognized that some countries had taken small actions to raise public awareness at national level but, so far, there had not been joint efforts across the region to combat SECT.

11. A professional, social marketing company named

Grey Worldwide, who had significant experience in behavior change campaigns, was selected for the production of the campaign. Under the overarching theme "Sex with children is a crime", it was agreed that the campaign would cover two different audiences:

(a) seven destination countries, targeting to local citizens, responsible tourists, expatriates, tourism industry and brothel patrons and,

(b) three sending countries, addressing potential offenders, family and friends of suspected offenders and general public.

According to the intention of making the campaign actionable, this project also involved the development of several reporting hotlines and the dissemination of stickers and posters translated into local languages which were placed in hotel rooms, internet cafes and photo shops. Ms. Dodds concluded that the Regional Campaign represented a good example of a partnership between eleven countries speaking with one voice to protect the tourism industry and to protect children from sexual exploitation in tourism.Presentation of Ms. Dodds.

12. Mr. Ignacio Angulo Ranz, Assistant Deputy Director General for Cooperation and Tourism Coordination of the General Secretariat for Tourism of Spain, presented the Campaign "Without Excuses" designed by UNICEF Spanish Committee with the financial support of the Ministry of Labour and Social Affairs, and which was integrated in the National Action Plan against sexual commercial exploitation of children. He said that some of the actions included the organization of meetings with tour operators, airlines and other tourism stakeholders, the participation in professional training seminars, the display of in-flight videos containing information on the campaign and the dissemination of a great number of posters, brochures and stickers. Mr. Angulo Ranz mentioned the Monographic

meeting on Tourism of the Spanish Council of Ministers held in 2005, in which the National government had endorsed the Global Code of Ethics for Tourism and had committed to its dissemination among the tourism industry in his country. Finally, he remarked that his government would prefer to discard the term "sexual tourism", since any criminal activity should be separated from the term "tourism", the latter being a legitimate activity that contributed to the economic development and mutual understanding among peoples and cultures around the world. Presentation of Mr. Angulo Ranz.

13. Mr. Philippe Kaspi, Adviser to the Minister of Tourism of France, mentioned several actions undertaken by the French Government since it decided to intensify the fight against sexual exploitation of children in tourism in the last two years. A working group composed by representatives from several ministries, organizations, NGOs and tourismcompanies had agreed to work on this issue in three main aspects: prevention, repression and international cooperation. He made reference to a Charter that had been signed between the Ministry of Tourism and the leading tourism companies in order to support the efforts of ECPAT France in implementing the Code of Conduct for the tourism industry. Furthermore, the Ministry of Tourism launched a proposal of a European Charter during the European Ministerial Meeting of Tourism in Malta that would enhance the actions started by the European Union in 1996. This French initiative would also include setting up an informal group with the participation of representatives of all Member States for the exchange of views and best practices as well as the development of an internal website with information on the situation in countries affected. Mr. Kaspi concluded that it was important to improve the international cooperation between receiving and sending countries and also to recognize that all stakeholders were involved in a long-lasting fight. French proposal against SECT

14. Ms. Angela Bähr, Project Director of the German Technical Cooperation (GTZ) reported on the Study of the Code of Conduct for the Protection of children from sexual exploitation in Travel and Tourism within the Context of Sustainability and Corporate Social Responsibility, aimed at developing standards and implementation criteria for social sustainability in the tourism sector. The approach of this project included somerecommendations for further action to build up a comprehensive concept of sustainability in tourism, comprising the protection of children's rights. She explained that this report identified some deficiencies on the implementation of the Code of Conduct, such as the differences between companies in the use of capacity-building materials and handbooks in tourism and also an insufficient integration of the Code in hotel contracts. The findings of the Study showed that companies should use their own management system as a starting point in the implementation of social standards and that they should cooperate with governmental and non governmental bodies. Finally, Ms. Bähr underlined that the priority of an implementation programme should be focused on the development of training activities involving train-the-trainer modules for auditors, staff of tourism companies, contractors and subcontractors and staff in destination countries. Presentation of Ms. Bähr.

Reporting Session

Reports on actions/measures taken by governments and organizations15.Mr. Yoshihisa Togo, Executive Director of UNICEF Japan Committee, reported on the situation of the Commercial Sexual Exploitation of Children in his country. The activities carried out to tackle this problem involved the establishment of a pressure group for the ratification of the Convention of the Rights of the Child by the Japanese Government, as well as awareness raising by means of public events and seminars. He further mentioned five Stockholm follow-up meetings and three signature-collection campaigns advocating the Japanese Government to establish laws against commercial sexual exploitation of children and trafficking. Mr. Togo indicated that thousands of posters and leaflets on this issue had been distributed, and that his country had hosted the Second World Congress against Commercial Sexual Exploitation of Children in Yokohama in 2001. He recalled their collaboration in the revision of the Act on Punishment for Child Prostitution, Child Pornography and Trafficking in Children for Sexual Purposes and on Protection and Care of Children in 2004. Finally, Mr. Togo reminded that the Code of Conduct was launched in Japan in 2005, and that it had been signed by major travel agencies and tour operators with the support of the Japan Association of Travel Agents which covered 90% of Japanese outbound tourism. Presentation of Mr. Togo.

16. Ms. Camelia Tepelus, Secretariat Coordinator of the Steering Committee of the Code of Conduct for the Protection of Children from Sexual Exploitation in Travel and Tourism, informed about the latest developments of the Code, which was represented in 23 countries and in more than 250 companies. She explained the Code criteria which constituted a set of six practical measures to be adopted by the private sector (tour operators, travel agencies, hotels). Some of the achievements during 2005 involved the signature of the Code in countries situated in Central and Eastern Europe (Romania, Bulgaria, Albania and Serbia and Montenegro) with the support of the Organization for Security and Cooperation in Europe. This effort in preventing the sexual exploitation of children in tourism had been joined by several travel associations and NGOs. The Code was also launched in Cancun, Mexico, within the framework of an ECPAT USA project funded by the US State Department where hotel and travel agency associations developed training programmes to build local capacity in order to prevent child sex tourism. Finally, Ms. Tepelus

explained the structure of the International Steering Committee composed by different stakeholders from the tourismindustry, international organizations, governments and NGOs. Presentation of Ms. Tepelus.

17. Mr. Chris Gould, Chief Superintendent of the Criminal Justice Department of the Avon and Somerset Constabulary in the United Kingdom, reported on Child Abuse within educational, cultural and language trips abroad. He introduced himself explaining that he was also the Chairman of the Board of Directors of the Child-Safe Charity aimed at protecting children and reducing crimes against children. The outcomes of several research projects that he conducted for many years showed that the sexual exploitation of children was not only a third world issue but it also happened in developed countries. He made reference to several US cases which prompted concern over exchange-student safety. The US Committee for Safety of Foreign Exchange Students had reported that over 18 months, 33 foreign exchange students living in the US had declared having been raped or abused by members of their host families. Mr. Gould also found that from 2000 cases of abuse of children placed in home-stays in 1998, only 1% had been reported to law enforcement agencies; the rest had been reported to tour operators, teachers or adults. No further action could, therefore, be taken and, consequently, there was a situation of under-reporting on this problem and very little information on the offenders.

18. Child-Safe Charity developed a website containing information on the different activities undertaken worldwide, and it published five books addressed to different audiences such as children, parents, host families, the voluntary sectors and schools. At national level, an Educational Visits Co-ordinator site focused on child protection issues was set up specifically for teachers in the UK who have a responsibility for sending young people across the world on different types of trips. Finally, Mr. Gould highlighted

some main actions that should be considered to improve the protection and reduce the exploitation of children in travel and tourism:

(a) raise awareness;
(b) fund-raising for the Child-Safe Charity and,
(c) lobbying the government to introduce a number of measures that would contribute to protect children. Presentation of Mr. Gould.

19. Ms. Susanna WILSON, Corporate Social Responsibility Manager of First Choice Holidays informed participants about some of the lessons learned from developing and implementing a training programme on protecting children from sexual exploitation. First Choice is one of the four big tour operators in the UK. It made a public commitment with sustainable development by taking a responsible approach with the environment and the local communities in tourism destinations. Ms. Wilson mentioned that they were promoting sustainable leisure travel and also training staff on how and on where to report suspected incidents, by identifying the most appropriate local NGOs to report to, which in turn would liaise with local police. She referred to the various activities that First Choice had undertaken together with ECPAT in the last years. With the support of the UK Charity Travel Foundation, the tour operator further produced a number of country profiles related to the current situation of sexual exploitation of children in Cuba, Bulgaria, The Gambia, Sri Lanka, Thailand and Mexico. Ms. Wilson stated that building local partnerships and networks with NGOs in tourism destinations would help preventing this practice in the future. Presentation of Ms. Wilson.

20. Ms. Rosa Martha Brown, Chairperson of the International Federation of Associations of Executive Women in Tourism, said that the efforts of professional women in the travel industry were aimed at involving the trade in

adopting social responsibility policies that would favor the adherence to a culture of protection of children's rights. She further referred to activities against SECT accomplished by the Infantia Foundation in Mexico, which participated in different projects in partnership with national and international organizations (ILO, UNICEF, UNWTO, ECPAT, Accor) in Mexico and the National Secretariat of Labour. Ms. Brown mentioned that the launch of a national awareness-raising campaign involved the dissemination of almost two million brochures and leaflets in Mexico city and Cancun airports, and that a number of workshops and training activities were organized for the travel industry, universities, unions and employees of the private sector in the framework of the International Program of Eliminating Child Labour (IPEC/ILO). Finally, Ms. Brown recognized that the creation of alliances between tourism stakeholders and the other sectors of society would improve the chances of children to live in dignity. Presentation of Ms. Brown.

21. At the end of the session, Ms Jacqueline de Rey, Honorary President of UFTAA, and Mr. Prathap Ramanujam, Permanent Secretary for Tourism of Sri Lanka, expressed their gratitude to UNWTO Deputy Secretary-General, Dr. Dawid de Villiers, for guiding the work of the Task Force during the last eight years. Because of his outstanding chairmanship, both members would propose and support Dr. de Villiers' continuity as Chairman of the Task Force beyond the mandate of the latter at UNWTO, due to come to an end in December 2005. After thanking the members for their kind words, Dr. de Villiers reminded the participants that it was up to the Secretary-General to designate the next Chairman of the Task Force.

Next Meeting

22. The Coordinator of the Task Force, Ms. Marina Diotallevi, announced that the eighteenth meeting of the Task Force was scheduled to take place at ITB Berlin, on 10 March 2006.

CODE OF CONDUCT: TOURISM QUEENSLAND

1. Introduction

This code of conduct is intended to give all Tourism Queensland staff a framework to assist us to continue projecting the professional image of this organisation.

In reading and implementing the code, we should also remember and take into consideration our Leadership Charter as well as the Ethics Principles for Public Officials.

Our leadership charter encourages us to lead by example, embrace change, be approachable, inspire a shared direction, empower others to act and respect the beliefs and values of others.

The ethics principles focus on respecting the law and the system of government, respect for persons, integrity, diligence and economy and efficiency.

Our Code of Conduct provides guidance about what is expected when performing our duties to ensure our decisions and behaviours are in line with the principles of public sector ethics and best practice.

2. Code of Conduct

2.1 Policy Statement

It is a fundamental principle of Tourism Queensland that all business dealings and interactions are conducted legally, ethically, with honesty and integrity. This code of conduct is based on that principle.

Why do we have a Code of Conduct?

Our Code of Conduct sets the standards expected of all Tourism Queensland staff. It provides information to assist in the understanding of the ethical values and standards of behaviour that apply in all of our daily business activities. These are the values and standards on which Tourism

Queensland?s reputation will be based. Adherence to these values is fundamental to building a partnership of trust between Tourism Queensland, industry, government and the community.

Who does the Code Apply To?

This code applies to all Tourism Queensland staff, from the Chairman and Chief Executive Officer to the newest employee. It also includes contractors, consultants and their employees. The code applies equally to all of us whether we are based in Brisbane Head Office, a Travel Centre or an international office.

What if the Code is not followed?

This code is applicable to all of us, and everyone is expected to follow the code. If the code is not followed, performance feedback will take place, with the outcomes of this feedback ranging from counselling to termination, depending on the severity of the breach. Where serious misconduct occurs, the incident may be referred to the Crime and Misconduct Commission for further investigation.

The code assumes the local laws, at all levels, are relevant to your place of work.

What do I do if I'm not sure?

We encourage you to discuss any contents of the code that you are not sure of with your supervisor, manager or a member of the Human Resources team.

What if I see someone else not following the code?

If you believe someone you work with is not following the code, we ask you to discuss this with either/and the person themselves, your supervisor, manager, a member of the Human Resources team or the Chief Executive Officer. The spirit of this code will enable you to discuss these issues without fear or risk of retribution.

Where else can I find relevant information?

If you have questions once you have read the code, other sources of relevant information include:

- — Financial Administration and Audit Act 1977
- — Financial Management Standard 1997
- — Public Sector Ethics Act 1994
- — Crime and Misconduct Act 2001
- — Tourism Queensland Act 1979
- — Whistleblowers Protection Act 1994
- — Tourism Queensland Financial Management Practice Manual
- — Tourism QueenslandHuman Resources Policy Manual
- — Tourism QueenslandTechnology Policies Manual

2.2 *Commissions and Payment Arrangements*

Commission and payment arrangements should only be made with companies, firms or individuals who are bona fide commercial representatives, agents or consultants.

You should ensure Tourism Queensland is not entering into arrangements with a company, firm or consultant where a government official or employee is known to have an interest. This may be allowed where prior approval is gained from the appropriate executive or the Chief Executive Officer.

A written contract or purchase order should exist for all commission and payment arrangements, and the payments should be reasonable and consistent with normal practice.

No payments should be made in cash.

2.3 *Business Documentation and Records*

Business documents (hard and soft copies) and records must not be destroyed prior to the statutory period requirements (please contact Financial and Business Services if you are unsure), and no records are to be falsified or manipulated.

Examples of some statutory periods include cash register strips, time sheets must be kept for 3 years official orders, bank deposit books and bank statements for 2 years.

2.4 Business Equipment

Business equipment in the form of, but not limited to computers, email, Internet and Voicemail is provided to enhance your ability to perform your role, and should not be used for personal gain.

The policy and procedures for each of these items are outlined within the Human Resources Policy and Procedures and Technology Policies and Procedures.

2.5 Community Activities

Tourism Queensland encourages its employees to participate in trade associations, professional associations, charitable or service organisations and other community activities.

We also understand that some employees may wish to participate in political activity and/or serve in public office. Due to Tourism Queensland being a statutory authority of the Queensland Government, if you wish to run for public office you will need to take leave from your position at Tourism Queensland. In the case of a state election, you will be deemed to vacate your position if you are successfully elected to office. If it is Federal Parliament you are standing for, you should resign from your position before nominating with the Australian Electoral Commission or run the risk of your election to a position being deemed invalid.

If you wish to participate in community activity we ask that you observe the following:

- — the time involved in these activities does not impact on your performance at Tourism Queensland
- — if the activity adversely affects your work performance, you may need to consider modifying the activity
- — where the activity is of a political nature, there should be no specific or implied Tourism Queensland endorsement of such activity
- — if you wish to speak at a public function, or write an Article in your own right, but not as an employee of Tourism Queensland, you must ensure Tourism Queensland information is not disclosed, Tourism Queensland logos and names do not appear (without express permission from the Corporate Communications Department), and when appropriate, indicate that you are not speaking as a representative of Tourism Queensland.

2.6 Company Property

Company assets, including goods, money, intellectual property or the services of other Tourism Queensland employees (including contractors), must not be used for personal gain. This includes, but is not limited to:

- — Transcription of computer software programs regardless of whether or not the programs are protected by copyright;
- — Falsification or improper use of corporate cards, expense accounts or other similar accounts.

Tourism Queensland property and merchandise is not to be removed from Tourism Queensland?s premises without authorisation. This includes any samples of merchandise received. If, for business reasons removal is necessary, then approval must be obtained from your supervisor.

Every employee while in control of any Tourism Queensland assets, particularly cash or other valuables, is personally accountable for them. If any item is lost, stolen or misplaced whilst under your control, please report this to Operations team of Financial and Business Services as soon as possible. We ask employees to take particular care with attractive items. For example, lap top computers should not be left in a visible position within an unoccupied vehicle.

2.7 Confidentiality

This confidentiality agreement applies to your existing position within Tourism Queensland, to any future position within Tourism Queensland and extends beyond the date of termination of your employment with Tourism Queensland.

You agree that you will not, either during or after your employment with Tourism Queensland, use or disclose confidential information or otherwise seek to exploit confidential information without the prior written consent of Tourism Queensland. You agree to prevent the use or disclosure of confidential information unless the information lawfully comes into the public domain through no fault of your own, or you are required to disclose the information by Tourism Queensland or by law. In this case you agree to give notice in writing to Tourism Queensland of any disclosure required by law.

Confidential Information includes oral, written, or conceptual information, of Tourism Queensland or its clients such as records, documents, accounts, plans, formulae, designs, creative concepts specifications, correspondence, letters and papers of every description. It also includes electronically recorded data, all copies or extracts relating to the affairs, transactions or business of Tourism Queensland or any of its clients or which may come into your possession during your employment with Tourism Queensland.

You acknowledge that, due to the nature of the duties and responsibilities of your employment with Tourism Queensland, you will be in possession of knowledge and documents, which will be strictly confidential and agree to preserve the private and confidential nature of such information with vigilance and diligence.

You will immediately notify Tourism Queensland of any use or disclosure by you of confidential information under the terms of this agreement.

You will keep Tourism Queensland fully and effectually indemnified in relation to all actions, claims and demands of whatsoever nature arising out of a breach of this agreement.

2.8 Conflict of Interest

A conflict of interest exists where loyalties are divided. You have a potential conflict of interest if, in the course of your work, any decision you make provides any improper gain or benefit to yourself or a third party.

Any situation potentially involving direct or indirect conflict of interest should be avoided unless consented to in writing by the Chief Executive Officer. The Board must consent to any situation potentially involving direct or indirect conflict of interest involving the Chief Executive Officer or any other director.

If you believe you know of a potential or actual conflict of interest you have a duty to raise that matter with your manager or to communicate your concerns to your director or the Chief Executive Officer.

It is impossible to formulate an all-embracing set of guidelines regarding potential conflicts of interest. Specific questions regarding situations not clearly covered must be determined on a case by case basis. The principles to consider are:

- Your capacity to influence dealings that Tourism Queensland may have with a third party;
- The improper personal benefit that may flow to you or a relative, friend or other third party through the exercise of that influence; and
- Whether the activity is fraudulent, corrupt or is an irregular transaction.

2.9 Declaration—Conflict of Interest

Where you believe you may have a conflict of interest or a potential conflict of interest, you must notify your supervisor in writing of that potential conflict and this will be forwarded to Human Resources. In specific circumstances we will ask for a declaration of conflicts from you as it may relate to a specific project you are working on.

This notification will be kept on your personnel file as well as in the Pecuniary Interest Register, (held in Human Resources) until we are notified by you that the association with the potential conflict no longer exits.

2.10 Disclosure of Information

Information may be disclosed to you or agents of Tourism Queensland who need to know the information to further Tourism Queensland?s interests, provided the disclosure does not breach any laws, regulations or Tourism Queensland policies. External disclosure of information should only be made with specific authorisation.

If you are unsure about whether it is appropriate to disclose information seek the permission of your immediate supervisor. There may be different delegations for dealing with different groups, such as the public, tourism industry members, government agencies, consultants and the media. Responsibility for ensuring that any disclosure is appropriate remains with the relevant supervisor.

Also refer to clause 2.7 Confidentiality.

2.11 Discrimination

Under our Employment Equity and Workplace Harassment Policy, Tourism Queensland is committed to providing all employees with equal opportunity.

Discrimination or harassment based on race, colour, religion, gender, age, marital status, disability or other factors unrelated to legitimate business interests, will not be tolerated. All applications for employment will be considered based on merit.

You are entitled to your personal preferences in private or political matters. No pressure will be placed on anyone to influence those preferences and no approval or disapproval should be shown by anyone in their Tourism Queensland role, of anybody?s private or political preferences or activities.

— Please refer to Sections 2 and 15 of the Human Resources Policy and Procedure Manual for more specific information.

2.12 Fraud, Corruption and Irregular Transactions

You must not engage in any unethical or improper payment practices either to obtain business or for personal gain. In particular you must not:

— engage in commercial bribery;
— be party to the bribery of public officials;
— establish so-called "slush funds" to facilitate bribery or other improper or questionable practices.

You will not be criticised for the loss of business resulting from not making or receiving a bribe or inducement to or from a third party.

You will be dismissed if you knowingly make or receive a bribe or inducement to or from a third party even if such a transaction is to further the cause of Tourism Queensland. Under no circumstances will a situation be tolerated where you benefit personally from such a transaction.

If you believe you know of any fraud, corruption, irregular transactions or breach of ethics you are required to raise that matter with your immediate supervisor or to communicate your concerns to your director or the Chief Executive Officer.

As part of its obligations under law, Tourism Queensland will fully co-operate with any investigation by law enforcement or regulatory authorities.

It will also require that you:

— do not make any disbursement of Tourism Queensland funds or other Tourism Queensland property without adequate supporting documentation. This includes ensuring that all appropriate payment authorisations are obtained in accord with delegated authorities. There shall be no disbursement for any purpose other than as described in the documents;
— do not make any direct or indirect personal payments to officials or employees of any government at any level with either Tourism Queensland funds or private funds;
— do not make any personal payments through Tourism Queensland accounts excluding payments of expenses which are later reimbursed to Tourism Queensland; and
— do not take any action or authorise any action, which involves illegal, unethical or otherwise improper payment of money or anything else of value.

2.13 *Giving and Receiving of Gifts*

Tourism Queensland upholds that its employees carry

out their roles impartially and with integrity. Consequently, it is not appropriate for employees to be offered or to accept or to give gifts and benefits that affect or may be likely to affect the performance of their duties.

Tourism Queensland employees must not ask for or encourage the giving of any form of gift or benefit in connection with the performance of official duties.

If a gift or benefit is offered, guidelines for acceptance or rejection of the offer and procedures for disclosure can be found in the Tourism Queesnland Giving and Receiving of Gifts Policy. This policy should not be seen as encouraging the receipt of gifts and benefits. However, where circumstances require the acceptance of a gift or benefit, it must occur in line with this policy. This policy also incorporates guidelines for the giving of gifts and benefits by employees.

The term Gifts and Benefits refers to items given and received in the course of official duties and includes (but is not limited to) gifts of money, alcohol, clothes, products, tickets, shares, travel, accommodation or access to a private spectator box at a sporting or other venue. It may also include promise of a new job or promotion, preferential treatment such as queue jumping, access to confidential information, use of facilities, hospitality or benefits generally.

There are three levels of gifts and benefits (nominal, significant and reportable). Within these levels gifts or benefits may be tangible (of lasting value) or intangible (of no lasting value). The same principles apply to all gifts and benefits; different procedures apply to different levels of gifts and benefits and intangible gifts and benefits.

Full details of the gift policy can be found in the Tourism Queensland Giving and Receiving of Gifts policy.

2.14 Internet and Email Usage

The use of communication and information devices must be lawful and appropriate and consistent with Tourism Queenslands Policy, as well as State and Federal legislation and regulations.

Some breaches of this policy may result in instant dismissal, in particular, downloading, storing and/or distributing pornography.

Full details of the internet policy can be found in the Tourism Queensland Phones, Email and Internet Policy

2.15 Leaving Tourism Queensland

On leaving Tourism Queensland you must surrender any Tourism Queensland assets and items containing business information. This includes intellectual property that may have been created while working with Tourism Queensland.

2.16 Outside Business Activities (Including Family and Friends)

Extreme care should be taken to ensure that active participation, on a part-time or freelance basis, in any outside business, whether or not such business is a supplier or client, does not create a potential conflict of interest.

If you are a full-time employee, and propose to engage in outside business activities, you should assess those activities in terms of the following guidelines to determine whether a conflict exists with your Tourism Queensland commitments:

— Where your participation in outside business activities interferes with your ability to satisfactorily perform assigned work for Tourism Queensland, a conflict of interest will exist;

- — Where, having knowledge of commercially sensitive information, you actively participate in outside business activities for a competitor of Tourism Queensland, a conflict of interest will exist;
- — Where you have knowledge of commercially sensitive information you shall not engage in any outside business activity for a supplier to Tourism Queensland without first obtaining written approval from your immediate supervisor;
- — Tourism Queensland will not accept any bid submitted by you to supply any goods, or perform any contract work for which tenders are sought, or negotiate contract work with you;
- — Where you actively participate in business activity for an outside company you may not render service to Tourism Queensland on that company's behalf.

2.17 Personal Conduct

Your personal conduct should be fully consistent with this code. You should deal fairly and honestly with each other, as well as with all external contacts.

All contacts should be handled professionally and courteously.

You should report to work as required and when an absence is unavoidable, promptly notify the appropriate person of the reason.

Any conduct that is intimidating or offensive to our clients, suppliers, contractors, the public or other employees will not be tolerated.

Please refer to the Enterprise Bargaining Agreement and the Performance Management Policy for more details.

2.18 Working Environment

Tourism Queensland will provide a safe, healthy and productive working environment. To this end the abuse of prescription drugs and/or alcohol or the use or possession of illicit drugs is not acceptable.

Neither is the consumption of alcohol where it affects your ability to perform your role, other employees, work performance, public relations, safety or where it violates the law.

Where the use of prescription drugs affects your ability to perform in your role, you should discuss this with your supervisor or Human Resources.

Tourism Queensland will provide confidential support to you if you require assistance in dealing with any substance abuse. Please contact Human Resources if you require assistance in this area.

Smoking on company premises is not permitted.

CODE OF ETHICS FOR KISKEYA ALTERNATIVE AND KALAU-DANZA

CODE OF CONDUCT FOR VISITORS IN AFRO-CARIBBEAN REGIONAL OF DOMENICAN REPUBLIC

Introduction

Kalalú-Danza that is a non for profit organization focusing on Afro-Caribbean identity revaluation, and conducts research and training activities as artistic performances and projects involving marginal communities and children.

It has created *Kiskeya Alternativa* as a program to use the Internet tools to enhance alternative tourism social, economical, cultural and environmental sustainability in the Dominican Republic and Haiti. By generating income out of tourism activities, Kiskeya Alternativa supports its activities and the projects of its umbrella organization Kalalú-Danza.

As a tour operator, Kiskeya Alternativa creates packages with different aspects, as culture nature and community. Community integration is a big issue in our developing of tourism products. We conceive alternative tourism as a conscious way of travelling, wherein open-minded travellers and host communities meet each other with mutual respect. In this meeting, traveller and host learn about each others social, cultural and environmental background. Alternative tourism is a personal search for real experiences and original entertainment away from the crowd in luxurious isolated resorts. It is about building paths oneself, while the traveller chooses where to stay and what to do and always looks for harmony with the hosting space.

To point out what we really stand for and to realize sustainable tourism development and community participation, we created a code of ethics for Kiskeya Alternativa and other collaborating organizations and a code of conducts for visitors.

Code of Ethics of Kiskeya Alternativa

Concerning Communities, Our Intentions are to:

- — Respect, valorize and not degrade the social, cultural, human and environmental background and values of the hosting community.
- — Promote involvement and active participation by community members in the project.
- — Empower community members to be actors of their own development process.
- — Bring direct financial benefit to the community or

bring resources for community development (infrastructure, education, organization skills, etc.).

— Keep social structure of host population intact by our activities and we avoid improper intrusions into their private lives.

— Try to use local supplies of accommodation, food and beverages and additional necessities as much as possible.

— Condemn any form of prostitution, vandalism or criminality.

Concerning Local Culture, Our Intentions are to:

— Protect the integrity of the culture and try to avoid visitor contribution to a decline of cultural values.

— Avoid using local culture and traditional expressions as a form of commercial merchandise but maintain and stimulate their original sources and authentic values.

— Enhance visitor understanding of the local culture and traditions and stimulate cross-cultural exchange between tourists and local residents so they learn about one another.

Concerning Natural Environment, Our Intentions are to:

— Avoid degradation and threatening of biological diversity, natural beauty and resources and landscape.

— Participate in efforts to protect and recover natural environment.

— Work with small groups at a time to reduce visitor impacts on the carrying capacity of the environment.

— Keep wildlife and habitats in (protected) natural areas intact.

— Use safe waste disposal in such content it doesn't damage natural environment.

Concerning Visitors

— We prepare travellers before departure, to minimize their negative impacts and maximize their positive impacts while visiting natural areas and local communities. We offer educational material to inform them about social structures, culture, history and environment. We have also a Code of Conduct for visitors.

— We maintain small groups of visitors to minimize group impact on the destination.

— We provide general travel ethics addressing standards for behaviour in natural areas and towards local culture.

— We encourage interaction between visitors and local communities while overseeing contact to avoid cultural errors.

— We give quality interpretation at all times in order to give visitors the proper background information.

Besides setting up these guidelines, we develop monitoring mechanisms so we can ensure the guidelines above are going to be applied.

Certification Program

Kiskeya Alternativa has developed a Tourism Sustainability Certification Program program with the objectives of (a) develop a tool to be sure to integrate in our project only partners (tourism operators) that meet minimal levels of sustainability on the environmental, social and cultural aspects (unfortunately in Dominican Rep. and Haiti anyone can today label itself as "ecotourism"); (b) develop and continue the process in collaboration with other institutions (environmental Ngos, academic, official) to build real and complete tool for establishing a National Certification Program; (c) Establish mechanisms for permanently monitor our integrated partners on their activities sustainability and "product quality".

A first tool was build up: The Tourism Sustainability Identification Questionnaire that you can access on line starting at our *Tourism Sustainability Certification Program* pages.

Code of Conducts for the Visitors

Kiskeya Alternativa is a local, responsible ecotour operator. We treat the environment, the culture and her members with the highest respect as stated in our Code of Ethics.

The Dominican Republic is a beautiful country with a great diversity of animals, flora and fauna and cultural sites. We ask you to help us to establish a harmony between people and the natural environment so that fragile habitats and places of cultural importance are conserved for our future generations.

By observing the next travel tips and following them you could only help preserve the Dominican environment and culture and upgrade your own quality of life.

- Natural environment and cultural sites
- About Prostitution and Discotheques
- Cultural and social travelling tips

In the Natural Environment and the Cultural Sites

- Leave only footprints. Take only photographs, no litter and don't take away 'souvenirs' from historical and natural areas.
- Show your respect for nature: keep to the proper

footpaths, don't feed wildlife, don't pick flowers or other vegetation and don't buy products made from endangered plants or animals

— Experience the environment by walking or other means and try to minimize the use of motorized transport.

— Move quietly and carefully as noise can disturb native birds, animals and reptiles, and in cultural places like churches.

— Put your litter in a bin or bring it home. Don't expect others to clean after you.

— Ask permission before photographing: at some historical and cultural places it is forbidden.

— Respect the privacy and dignity of others.

— Permission may be required to visit some cultural sites.

— Consider the privacy, cultural heritage, habits and traditions of the host community: dress properly before entering historical sites: suitable wear for women then should be a skirt beneath the knees or trousers and sleeveless shirts aren't desired. Haitians and Dominicans are used to dress conservatively: try to dress to these standards. Beachwear should never be worn away from the beach or poolside, skirts above the knee are considered risqué and men should wear a shirt away from the beachside.

— When taking pictures, respect the privacy of others: ask permission and use restraint.

— Remove litter and don't pollute

— Water is scarce in the country so practice conservation and avoid pollution

— The drain system here is different from which we are used to: try to avoid throwing toilet paper into the toilets.

— Place your litter in a dustbin or carry it home.
— Observe local fire restrictions and be careful with cigarettes butts and matches.
— Use energy efficiently

About Prostitution and Discotheques

— Unfortunately sex tourism also appears in the Dominican Republic, and is mostly presented in the beach areas. To avoid any problems or encourage their business they are practising, don't get involved with these people.
— The manners in discotheques are a bit different compared to western standards. It isn't common for Dominican women to go out alone. If they do, you can assume they are pleasure girls and want something of you. To avoid problems, always be careful if you ask Dominican women to dance. When you go out with Dominican boys, always make clear that you want nothing more of them than just having a nice time.

Cultural and Social Travelling Tips

— Learn about the geography, customs, manners and culture of the island. Take time to listen to the people and encourage local conservation efforts. Share your own stories, help them the locals to gain a realistic view of life in Western Countries.
— Support the local economy by buying local goods and services.
— Giving money to beggars only encourages their begging. If you really want to help them, give a donation to a project, school or health centre. It is a more constructive way to help.
— Get used to hearing 'gringo/a', 'rubio/a' shouted at you. Don't take it as an insult; it is a generic term

for 'foreigner' rather than a jibe at your colour. Most of the time it is intended as a greeting, and a smile is a welcome reply.

— Don't get involved with any kind of illegal drugs, as a foreigner you are always at a distinct disadvantage. The local police will be very harsh on foreigners.

— By following these guidelines you will help to protect the environment, enjoy you stay at the utmost and we all pull together to preserve it for future visitors.

NATIONAL TOUR ASSOCIATION, INC. , KENTUCKY, USA

Preamble

National Tour Association, Inc. ("NTA") is a Kentucky non-profit, trade association. NTA's principal purpose is to promote and foster national and international public interest in Packaged Travel and the mutual interests of those engaged in conducting the business of, and businesses for or associated with, Packaged Travel. The business and affairs of NTA are managed under the direction of the Board of Directors ("Board") and the Officers of NTA. This Board of Directors and Officer's Code of Ethics and Conflict of Interest Policy ("Code") serves as a code of conduct for members of the Board and Officers in their capacity as such. Violations of the Code may result in sanctions imposed under the Procedures for Review of Directors and Officer Conduct ("Procedures").

The principles and requirements that comprise this Code and the Procedures are based upon, and are designed to, assist (and not to supersede, limit or extend) in compliance by NTA and its Directors and Officers with the fiduciary duties imposed upon such individuals by the laws of the

Commonwealth of Kentucky, the federal tax code's prohibition on private inurement and private benefit and other requirements of federal tax exemption, common law due process requirements, federal and state antitrust and unfair competition law, state tort law, and other legal precepts and prohibitions. Moreover, the checks and balances built into the Code and Procedures are designed to strike the proper balance between ensuring full compliance with the legal obligations described above and ensuring the integrity and efficacy of the Code on the one hand, and protecting Directors and Officers, through the use of reasonable due process procedures, against patently false, malicious or groundless accusations that could result in significant business or personal harm if not properly handled.

A person by accepting nomination and election or appointment, as the case may be, to the position of Director or Officer of NTA, affirms his or her endorsement of the Code and Procedures and acknowledges his or her commitment to uphold his or her principles and obligations under the Code.

The interpretation and application of the Code and Procedures are to be under the laws of the Commonwealth of Kentucky.

NTA Board of Directors and Officers Code of Ethics

Members of the NTA Board (including ex officio members of the Board) and Officers of NTA shall, at all times, abide by and conform to the following Code in their capacity as Directors and Officers:

1. Each NTA Director and Officer, shall abide in all respects by the Code, NTA's Code of Ethics and Professional Responsibility and all other rules and regulations of NTA (including but not limited to NTA's Articles of Incorporation and Bylaws, as amended) and shall ensure that his or her NTA

membership, or the NTA membership of the entity which entitles such NTA Director or Officer to serve as such, remains in good standing at all times. Each Director and Officer shall, at all times, obey all applicable federal, state and local laws and regulations and shall provide or cause to provide the full cooperation of NTA when requested to do so by those institutions and their persons set in authority as are required to uphold the law.

2. Each Director and Officer shall conduct and participate in the business and affairs of NTA in good faith and with honesty, integrity, due diligence, discretion, due respect for confidentiality and reasonable competence.
3. A Director or Officer should not, in the regular course of business, disclose information about the NTA's activities, unless the same is already known by the public or of public record or is required by law, except as the Board and Officers may otherwise specifically instruct. Specifically, no Director or Officer shall share, copy, reproduce, transmit, divulge or otherwise disclose any confidential information related to the affairs of NTA, and each Director and Officer shall uphold the strict confidentiality of all meetings and other deliberations and communications of the Directors and Officers. In the normal course of business, a Director or Officer should treat, as confidential, all matters involving NTA until there has been general public disclosure or unless the information is a matter of public record or common knowledge. An individual Director or individual Officer (except for the Chairman and CEO and President, and who are recognized as the spokespersons for NTA,

and the NTA Senior Vice-President – Communications, and the NTA Director of Governmental Relations, and designated members of NTA Staff, whose everyday assigned duties include making public statements in their assigned areas) is not a spokesperson for NTA and shall not make disclosures to the public of NTA activities.

4. Each Director and Officer shall exercise proper authority, courtesy and good judgment in their dealings with NTA staff, NTA Members, NTA contractors and the general public and shall respond to the needs of NTA's members in a responsible, respectful and professional manner.
5. No Director or Officer shall use any information provided by NTA, or acquired as a consequence of the Director's or Officer's service to the NTA, in any manner other than in furtherance of his or her duties. No Director or Officer shall misuse NTA property or resources and shall, at all times, keep NTA's property secure and not allow any person not authorized by the Board to have or use such property.
6. Each Director and Officer shall use his or her best efforts to regularly participate in professional development activities and shall perform his or her assigned duties in a professional and timely manner pursuant to the Board's direction and oversight.
7. Each Director and Officer dedicates himself or herself to leading by example in serving the needs of NTA and all of its members (and not just the particular constituency that elected him or her), and in representing the interests and ideals of the travel and tourism industry at large.

8. No Director or Officer shall persuade or attempt to persuade any member of NTA Staff or employee of a contractor of NTA to leave his or her current employment or to become employed by any person or entity other than NTA (and, in the case of NTA, only in the event the employer [or its controlling parent entity] of the NTA Staff Member or employee of a contractor of NTA is in insolvency or bankruptcy proceedings). Furthermore, no Director or Officer shall persuade or attempt to persuade any member, exhibitor, advertiser, sponsor, subscriber, supplier, contractor or any other person or entity, with an actual or potential relationship to or with NTA, or with a contractor to NTA, to terminate, curtail or not enter into its relationship to or with NTA, or to, in any way, reduce the monetary or other benefits to NTA of such relationship.
9. Each Director and Officer shall act, at all times, in the best interests of NTA and not for personal or third-party gain or financial enrichment. The responsibility to identify a potential conflict of interest lies with an Officer of Director. When encountering potential conflicts of interest, a Director or Officer, himself or herself, shall identify the conflict and, as required, remove himself or herself from all discussion and voting on the matter. Generally, Directors and Officers shall:

— avoid placing (and avoid the appearance of placing) one's own self-interest or any third-party interest above that of NTA (while the receipt of incidental personal or third-party benefit may necessarily flow from certain NTA activities, such benefit must be merely incidental to the primary benefit to NTA and its purposes);

— not abuse their position as a Director or Officer by improperly using their status as such, or NTA's staff, services, equipment, resources or property for their personal or third-party gain or pleasure, and not represent to third-parties that their authority as a Director or Officer extends any further than that which it actually extends;

— not engage in any outside business, professional or other activities that would directly or indirectly materially adversely affect NTA;

— not engage in or facilitate any discriminatory, abusive or harassing behavior directed toward NTA staff, members, Officers, Directors, meeting attendees, exhibitors, advertisers, sponsors, suppliers, contractors or others in the context of activities relating to NTA;

— notwithstanding that NTA recognizes and acknowledges that it is customary and acceptable for the members of the tour and travel industry and travel press to exchange and/or accept complimentary travel and tourism services (i.e. lodging, travel services, meals, attraction admissions and the like), no Director of Officer shall solicit or accept gifts, gratuities, free trips, honoraria, personal property or any other item of value from any person or entity (i) as direct or indirect inducement to provide special treatment to such donor with respect to matters pertaining to NTA; or (ii) in excess of $500.00 in value, or in a single instance, aggregating to in excess of $500.00 in value, without fully disclosing the receipt of such travel and tourism services to the Executive Committee within thirty (30) days of the receipt thereof; and not provide goods or services to NTA, as a paid vendor to NTA, unless full disclosure to, and advance approval by, the Board has been obtained, and pursuant to any related procedures adopted by the Board.

NTA BOARD OF DIRECTORS AND OFFICERSCONFLICT OF INTEREST POLICY

Article I

Preamble

The purpose of the Code's conflict of interest policy is to protect NTA's interest when it is contemplating entering into a transaction or arrangement that might benefit the private interest of an Officer or Director of NTA. This policy is intended to supplement, but not replace, any applicable state and federal laws governing conflict of interest applicable to nonprofit and charitable organizations.

Article II

Definitions

1. Interested Person

Any Director or Officer of NTA who has a direct or indirect Financial Interest, as defined below, is an Interested Person.

2. Financial Interest

A person has a Financial Interest if the person has, directly or indirectly, through business, investment, or family relationship:

(a) An ownership or investment interest in any entity with which NTA has a transaction or;

(b) A compensation arrangement with NTA or with any entity or individual with which NTA has a transaction or arrangement;

(c) A potential ownership or investment interest in, or compensation arrangement with, any entity or individual with which NTA is negotiating a transaction or arrangement; or

(d) An ownership or investment interest in any entity with which an NTA Principal Contractor has a transaction or arrangement.

Compensation includes direct and indirect remuneration, as well as gifts or favors that are not insubstantial.

A Financial Interest is not necessarily a conflict of interest. Under Article III, Section 2, a person who has a Financial Interest may have a conflict of interest only if the Board or appropriate committee decides that a conflict of interest exists. In this regard it is specifically recognized, acknowledged, and agreed that the President of NTA is an employee of Host Communications, Inc. [an NTA Principal Contractor] and as such will have an employment relationship, and an ownership interest in Host Communications, Inc., and that the President of NTA's Financial Interest in Host Communications, Inc., does not in and of itself constitute a conflict of interest.

Article III

Procedures

1. Duty to Disclose

In connection with any actual or possible conflict of interest, an Interested Person shall disclose the existence of the Financial Interest and all material facts, to the Board of Directors.

2. Determining Whether a Conflict of Interest Exists

After disclosure of the Financial Interest and all material facts, and after any discussion with the Interested Person, he/she shall leave the Board of Directors meeting while the determination of a conflict of interest is discussed and voted upon. The remaining Board of Directors members shall decide if a conflict of interest exists.

3. Procedures for Addressing the Conflict of Interest

(a) An Interested Person may make a presentation at the Board of Directors, but after the presentation, he/she shall leave the meeting during the discussion of, and the vote on, the transaction or arrangement involving the possible conflict of interest.

(b) The Chairman of NTA shall, if appropriate, appoint a disinterested person or committee to investigate alternatives to the proposed transaction or arrangement.

(c) After exercising due diligence, the Board of Directors shall determine whether NTA can obtain, with reasonable efforts, a more advantageous transaction or arrangement from a person or entity that would not give rise to a conflict of interest.

(d) If a more advantageous transaction or arrangement is not reasonably possible under circumstances not producing a conflict of interest, the Board of Directors shall determine, by a majority vote of thedisinterested directors, whether the transaction or arrangement is in NTA's best interest for its own benefit, and whether it is fair and reasonable conformity with the above determination, it shall make its decision as to whether to enter into the transaction or arrangement.

4. Violations of the Conflicts of Interest Policy

(a) If the Board of Directors has reasonable cause to believe a Director or Officer has failed to disclose actual or possible conflicts of interest, it shall inform the Director or Officer of the basis for such belief and afford such person an opportunity to explain the alleged failure to disclose.

(b) If, after hearing the Director or Officer's response, and after making further investigation as warranted by the circumstances, the Board of Directors determines the Director or Officer has failed to disclose an actual or possible conflict of interest, it shall take appropriate disciplinary and corrective action.

Article IV

Records of Proceedings

The minutes of the Board of Directors considering a Financial Interest in connection with an actual or potential conflict of interest shall contain:

(a) The names of the persons who disclosed or otherwise were found to have a Financial Interest in connection with an actual or possible conflict of interest, the nature of the Financial Interest, any action taken to determine whether a conflict of interest was present, and the Boardof Director's decision as to whether a conflict of interest in fact existed.

(b) The names of the persons who were present for discussions and votes relating to the transaction or arrangement, the content of the discussion, including any alternatives to the proposed transaction or arrangement, and a record of any votes taken in connection with the proceedings.

Article V

Annual Statements

Each Director and Officer shall annually sign and deliver a statement with NTA which:

(a) Affirms such person has received a copy of this Code;

(b) Affirms such person has read and understands this Code;

(c) Affirms such person has agreed to comply with this Code;

(d) Affirms such person understands that NTA is a non-profit trade association in order to maintain its federal tax exemption it must engage primarily in activities which accomplish one or more of its tax-exempt purposes; and

(e) Identifies and sets forth:

(i) All trade associations in which the Director or Officer holds a management or leadership position; and

(ii) all business entities engaged in the travel and tourism industry in which the Director or Officer directly or indirectly holds/owns an equity interest.

NATIONAL TOUR ASSOCIATION, INC.

Membership Requirements and Standards

The National Tour Association, Inc. ("NTA") has adopted By-Laws which authorize the Board of Directors from time to time to establish as a part of the By-laws, requirements and standards for a Person's eligibility for the classes of membership of NTA. Pursuant to the By-laws of the NTA, the Board of Directors has adopted these requirements and standards for a Person's eligibility for the classes of membership of NTA, which are incorporated into and made a part of NTA's By-laws, as follows1:

1.0 Tour Operator Membership

1.1 Requirements and Standards

A Person which complies with the following requirements and standards is eligible for membership and to continue such Person's membership, as a Tour Operator Member of the Corporation:

A. The Person shall actively and on an ongoing basis, as a "Tour Operator", engage in the business of developing, packaging, producing, promoting, selling and operating Packaged Travel of the Tour Operator on a for-profit basis.

B. The Person shall be in compliance with all applicable laws, rules and regulations, and be duly qualified and licensed to do business in each jurisdiction which requires such qualification or licensing.

C. The Person shall have, in a senior management position, on a full-time basis (30 hours or more per week), an individual Person who has been actively engaged in the business of developing, packaging, promoting, selling and operating Packaged Travel for at least three years immediately prior to the date of such Person's application for Tour Operator Membership.

D. In the event the Person's principle business office is located in North America,(A) the Person shall maintain (and provide NTA with satisfactory evidence of maintenance), with a reputable insurance underwriting company or through a proven self-insurance fund (proof regarding any Person's self-insurance fund shall be provided annually in a form prescribed by the Board of Directors to include documentation derived from independent annual audits), comprehensive general public liability insurance coverage of the Person's operations, with minimum coverage limits of $1,000,000.00 USD aggregate annually; AND (B) the Person

(1) shall I Initial capitalized terms used herein, not otherwise used herein, have the meanings assigned to them in the bylaws. maintain (and provide NTA with satisfactory evidence of maintenance), with a reputable insurance underwriting company or through a proven self-insurance fund (proof regarding any Person's self-insurance fund shall be provided annually in a form prescribed by the Board of Directors to include documentation derived from independent annual audits), professional errors and omissions insurance coverage of the Person's employees and operations, with minimum coverage limits of $1,000,000.00 USD aggregate annually, or

(2) shall maintain (and provide NTA with satisfactory evidence of maintenance), with a reputable insurance underwriting company or through a proven self-insurance fund (proof regarding any Person's self-insurance fund shall be provided annually in a form prescribed by the Board of Directors to include documentation derived from independent annual audits), hired non-owned automobile/motorcoach liability insurance coverage for the Person's operations, with minimum coverage limits of $1,000,000.00 USD aggregate annually, or

(3) shall on a rolling and moving forward basis, maintain a three year history of active engagement in the business of developing, packaging, promoting, selling and operating Packaged

Travel, or (4) shall operate, maintain, and utilize (and provide NTA with a satisfactory statement/ verification of the Person's operation, maintenance and use) of a Consumer Deposit Trust Account, with a reputable financial institution (for US Tour Operators, a FDIC insured and protected financial institution), for the deposit, withdrawal and use of funds received from the Person's customers, in form approved by and acceptable to NTA, or (5) shall maintain (and provide NTA with satisfactory evidence of maintenance), a certification of a quality management system meeting the requirements of ISO 9001-2000 as established by IQ NET Association, Bern, Switzerland and/or one of its partner organizations, or (6) shall provide (and provide NTA with a satisfactory statement/ verification of the Person's compliance), each and every of the Person's customers with comprehensive travel protection insurance (i.e. trip cancellation and trip interruption insurance), underwritten by a reputable insurance company.

E. In the event the Person's principal business office is located outside North America, the Person shall satisfy any two of the following standards:

(1) the Person shall maintain (and provide NTA with satisfactory evidence of maintenance), with a reputable insurance underwriting company, comprehensive general public liability insurance coverage of the Person's operations, with coverage limits in amounts as determined by the President of NTA or his/her designee to be reasonable or appropriate under the circumstances (the President or his/her designee

shall, as a benchmark, require coverage amounts of $1,000,000.00 USD annually, or the equivalents thereof [i.e., a bond]; however, the President of NTA of his/her designee is authorized to deviate from this benchmark if, in his/her judgment, the circumstances of the Person deem it appropriate to deviate from the benchmark of $1,000,000.00 aggregate annually);

(2) the Person shall maintain (and provide NTA with satisfactory evidence of maintenance), with a reputable insurance underwriting company, professional errors and omissions insurance coverage of the Person's employees and operations, with coverage limits in amounts as determined by the President of NTA or his/her designee to be reasonable or appropriate under the circumstances (the President or his/her designee shall, as a benchmark, require coverage amounts of $1,000,000.00 USD annually, or the equivalents thereof [i.e., a bond]; however, the President of NTA of his/her designee is authorized to deviate from this benchmark if, in his/her judgment, the circumstances of the Person deem it appropriate to deviate from the benchmark of $1,000,000.00 aggregate annually);

(3) the Person shall maintain (and provide NTA with satisfactory evidence of maintenance), with a reputable insurance underwriting company, hired non-owned automobile/motorcoach liability insurance coverage for the Person's operations, with coverage limits in amounts as determined by the President of NTA or his/her designee to be reasonable or appropriate under the circumstances (the President or his/her

designee shall, as a benchmark, require coverage amounts of $1,000,000.00 USD annually, or the equivalents thereof [i.e., a bond]; however, the President of NTA of his/her designee is authorized to deviate from this benchmark if, in his/her judgment, the circumstances of the Person deem it appropriate to deviate from the benchmark of $1,000,000.00 aggregate annually);

(4) shall on a rolling and moving forward basis, maintain a three year history of active engagement in the business of developing, packaging, promoting, selling and operating Packaged Travel;

(5) shall operate, maintain, and utilize (and provide NTA with a satisfactory statement/verification of the Person's operation, maintenance and use) of a Consumer Deposit Trust Account, with a reputable financial institution, for the deposit, withdrawal and use of funds received from the Person's customers, in form approved by and acceptable to NTA;

(6) shall maintain (and provide NTA with satisfactory evidence of maintenance), a certification of a quality management system meeting the requirements of ISO 9001-2000 as established by IQ NET Association, Bern, Switzerland and/or one of its partner organizations;

(7) shall maintain (and provide NTA with satisfactory evidence of maintenance), membership in good standing in an established and recognized, national or international travel trade association as determined by the President of NTA or his/her designee to be so established

and recognized (i.e. and without limitation Deutscher Reisebuero Verband [DRV], Association of British Travel Agents [ABTA], British Incoming Tour Operators Association [BITOA], European Travel Commission [ETC]); and/or

(8) shall provide (and provide NTA with a satisfactory statement/verification of the Person's compliance), each and every of the Person's customers with comprehensive travel protection insurance (i.e. trip cancellation and trip interruption insurance), underwritten by a reputable insurance company.

F. The Person shall provide a satisfactory statement/verification of financial stability, in form approved by and acceptable to NTA.

G. The existence of any one or more of the following events during the five (5) years immediately preceding the date of a Person's application for Tour Operator Membership may be grounds for denial of Tour Operator Membership to the Person:

(1) A petition under federal, national, or state/provincial bankruptcy laws or any federal, national, or state/provincial insolvency law having been filed by or against, or a receiver, fiscal agent, or similar officer having been appointed by a court for the business or property of the Person, or any Person in which the Person was a general partner, executive officer, officer, director, or 10% or more partner, member, shareholder or equity participant, at or within two years before the time of such filing;

(2) The Person was convicted of a felony or is the subject of a pending criminal felony proceeding; or

(3) The Person has demonstrated a disregard for the principles to truth, accuracy, fairness and integrity as reflected in the Corporation's Code of Ethics and Professional Responsibility.

H. In the event a Person applies for Tour Operator Membership to operate under an identity (name) or identities other than the Person's own true legal identity as an NTA member tour operator, the Person shall submit documentation of rights under its local law to use such other identity or identities. Both the true legal identity of the Person and the other identity or identities to be used by the Person shall be submitted to the Membership for comments.

For the purposes hereof, the Person shall include not only the Person applying for Tour Operator Membership, but also all of the Person's Directors, Officers, Beneficial Owners and the individual or individuals in a senior management position whose employment qualified the Person for Tour Operator Membership. A Person or individual will be considered to be a Beneficial Owner of the Person applying for Tour Operator Membership if the Person or individual owns a 10% or more equity interest in the Person applying for Tour Operator Membership, either in the Person's or individual's own name, or in the name of others for the benefit of such Beneficial Owner.

1.2 Status of Tour Operator Membership After Transfer of Ownership Interest in Tour Operator Member, Transfer of Substantially all of Tour Operator Member's Business and Assets, or Transfer of a Substantial Portion of Tour Operator's Business and Assets to an Affiliate of the Tour Operator

A. Unless the equity securities of a Tour Operator Member have been registered with a governmental authority for public trading on a recognized securities market and are publicly traded on a recognized securities market, in the event that there is a change of fifty percent (50%) or more in the equity ownership of a Tour Operator Member, from the time of the Tour Operator Member's original application for Tour Operator Membership, or previous approval of transfer, the Tour Operator Member shall be required to obtain approval by two-thirds (2/3) vote of the Board of Directors for the continuance of its Tour Operator Membership. It is the responsibility of each Tour Operator Member to report to the Corporation any change of fifty percent (50%) or more in the Tour Operator Member's equity ownership. A request for continuance of Tour Operator Membership must be submitted as a new application and the transfer of ownership in a Tour Operator Membership will be submitted to the Membership of the Corporation for comment. Unless the Corporation's staff has received the necessary information to cause the application for continuance of Tour Operator Membership to be completely processed within one hundred twenty (120) days from the date of ownership change, the Tour Operator Membership of the Tour Operator Member will be automatically terminated; provided, however an extension of this period may be granted by the President of the Corporation, or his designee, for good cause shown.

B. In the event that substantially all of the business and assets of a Tour Operator Member are transferred to a non-member, the Tour Operator Member's membership in NTA shall terminate and except as specifically provided herein below, such non-member shall not be entitled to a transfer of the Tour Operator Membership, however may apply for Tour Operator Membership and be admitted to Tour Operator Membership if the non-member meets all standards and requirements for Tour Operator Membership set forth herein. The President of the Corporation, or his designee, may grant a temporary transfer of Tour Operator Membership to the non-member for a period of up to one hundred twenty (120) days and the Board of Directors, to the extent that it is deemed appropriate, due to the continuation of the same or related ownership, the retention in the business of senior management or other related factors, may grant a full transfer of the Tour Operator Membership to said non-member.

In the event that a substantial portion, but not all of the business and assets of a Tour Operator Member are transferred to a non-member Affiliate of the Tour Operator Member and the Tour Operator Member retains sufficient business, senior management, and assets to meet all standards for Tour Operator Membership, as if made applicable to the retained portion of business, senior management, and assets, such non-member Affiliate of the Tour Operator Member may apply for Tour Operator Membership and be admitted to Tour Operator Membership if the non-member Affiliate of the Tour Operator meets all standards and requirements for Tour Operator Membership set forth herein. The President of the Corporation, or his designee, may grant a temporary Tour Operator Membership to the non-member Affiliate of the Tour Operator Member-Transferor referred to herein, for a period of up to one hundred twenty (120) days and the Board of Directors, to the extent that it is deemed appropriate, due to the continuation of indirect equitable ownership, the employment of senior management by the non-member Affiliate of the Tour Operator Member-Transferor which was previously employed by the Tour Operator Member-Transferor or other related factors, may grant a full transfer of the Tour Operator Membership to said non-member Affiliate of the Tour Operator Member-Transferor.

1.3 Applications for Membership of Persons Who Have Been Removed From Membership in NTA for Cause

A Person who has been removed from Membership in NTA by action of the Board of Directors (i) for any violation of NTA's Code of Ethics and Professional Responsibility or (ii) for conduct or business practices which adversely affect the travel industry, may reapply for membership in NTA no sooner than three (3) years after the effective date of such Member's removal from Membership in NTA. The Board of Directors of NTA shall consider such Persons application for Membership in NTA at a regular or special meeting of the Board of Directors; and at such meeting, shall consider the facts that resulted in such Person's removal from Membership in NTA and shall consider developments occurring since such Person's removal from Membership in NTA.

Any Person who has been removed from Membership in NTA (i) for any violation of NTA's Code of Ethics and Professional Responsibility or (ii) for conduct or business practices which adversely affect the travel industry, shall have the opportunity to present, in person, at the regular or special meeting of the Board of Directors at which such Person's application for Membership in NTA is considered, all developments and other information occurring since such Person's removal from Membership, pertinent to such Person's application for Membership in NTA.

2.0 Tour Supplier Membership

A Person which is engaged in the business of marketing or providing Packaged Travel components, and is in compliance with all applicable laws, rules, regulations and is duly qualified and licensed to do business in each jurisdiction from which requires such qualifications or licensing, is eligible for membership and to continue its membership as a Tour Supplier Member of the Corporation.

3.0 Destination Marketing Organization Membership

A Person which is a destination marketing organization for a city, state/province, region or country, is a non-profit organization, whose primary purpose is the promotion of the city, state/province, region or country and is representative of at least three (3) of the multiple components (i.e. lodging, attractions, restaurants, etc.) of the travel and tourism industry within a city, state/province, region or country, is eligible for membership, and to continue its membership, as a Destination Marketing Organization Member of the Corporation.

4.0 Associate Membership

A Person which provides a product or service that enhances the quality or safety of tour operation and is in compliance with all applicable laws, rules, regulations, and is duly qualified and licensed to do business in each jurisdiction which requires such qualifications or licensing, is eligible for membership and to continue its membership as an Associate Membership of the Corporation. Provided however, Associate Membership is not available to any Person which is eligible for membership in another category of membership as outlined in the By-Laws.

5.0 Educator Membership

A Person or individual which is an educational group or representative of such, which or whom engages in educational or research activities in the areas of travel and tourism, is eligible for membership and to continue its membership, as an Educator Member of the Corporation. Provided however, individual Educator Members must be actively employed by a certified educational or diploma granting institution and there shall be a limit of one individual Member from each such institution; and non-individual Educator Members must be accredited or licensed to operate under appropriate governmental authority.

6.0 Alumni Membership

A Person or individual which complies with the following requirements and standards is eligible for membership and to continue its membership, as an Alumni Membership of the Corporation:

A. The Person is retired from a Tour Operator business and was a principal officer, sole proprietor, or 10% or more equity partner, member or shareholder, and a designated representative of a Tour Operator Member, which was an NTA Tour Operator Member for at least five (5) years; or

B. The Person is retired from employment with a current Tour Supplier Member or Destination Marketing Organization Member, which had been an Tour Supplier Member or Destination Marketing Organization Member, for at least ten (10) years, and who (i) has had a minimum of fifteen (15) years of involvement or experience in the tourism industry, (ii) is not employed in any capacity by any Person that is eligible to become a Member of any class of Membership of NTA, or any Person which is in competition with a Member of any class of Membership of NTA, and (iii) has provided two letters of reference, one from the Person from which the proposed Member has retired, if it is still in existence, and one from a current Member in the NTA Membership category from which the proposed Member has retired.

7.0 Honorary Membership

The Board of Directors may confer Honorary Membership upon any Person or individual who, in the judgment of the Board is suitable for recognition as an Honorary Member.

8.0 Dues and Admissions Fees for Classes of Membership of NTA

The annual dues and admissions fees for the classes of Membership of NTA, for 2006 and subsequent years are as follows:

A. Tour Operator Membership:
   1. Admission Fee: $ -0- U.S.
   2. Annual Dues: $ 450.00 U.S.

B. Tour Supplier Membership:
   1. Admission Fee: $ 350.00 U.S.
   2. Annual Dues:
      (a) Representative of 1 Property: $ 615.00 U.S.
      (b) Representative of 2 to 25 Properties: $ 965.00 U.S.
      (c) Representative of in excess of 25 Properties: $1,690.00 U.S.

C. Destination Marketing Organization Membership:
   1. Admission Fee: $ 350.00 U.S.
   2. Annual Dues: $ 615.00 U.S.

D. Associate Membership:
   1. Admission Fee: $1,000.00 U.S.
   2. Annual Dues: $ 325.00 U.S.

E. Educator Membership:
   1. Admission Fee: $1,000.00 U.S.
   2. Annual Dues: $ 125.00 U.S.

F. Alumni Membership:
   1. Admission Fee: $ 0.00 U.S.
   2. Annual Dues: $ 50.00 U.S.

G. Honorary Membership:
   1. Admission Fee: $ 0.00 U.S.
   2. Annual Dues: $ 0.00 U.S.

9.0 Filing of a Petition Under the Applicable Federal, State, National, Provincial or Local Laws By or Against a Member

In the event that the President, or his designee, determines that the provisions of the By-Laws of NTA providing for the Automatic Termination of the Membership of a Member may have been or will be superseded by applicable federal, state, national, provincial, or local bankruptcy or insolvency laws, the President, or his designee, may alternatively, for good cause shown, declare the Member's NTA Membership to be classified as "Pending/De-Activated". The classification of a NTA Membership as "Pending/De-activated" shall result in a temporary moratorium on all membership privileges of such Member. A Member whose NTA Membership has been classified as "Pending/De-activated" may apply to the Board of Directors for re-classification as a full NTA Member with all attendant privileges and benefits, by setting forth and making an application to NTA, containing all information, and documents required under NTA's By-Laws and these Membership Requirements and Standards for the Member's membership category. The Board of Directors in evaluating the Member's Application, shall give due consideration to all relevant factors.

10.0 Standards for NTA Member's Representatives/ Delegates at NTA Conventions and/or NTA Spring Meets

No NTA Member, without the prior written approval of NTA, shall designate any individual Person as such NTA Member's representative/delegate, to attend a NTA Convention and/or a NTA Spring Meet:

A. For whom, within the past five (5) years immediately preceding the NTA Convention and/or NTA Spring Meet, (i) a petition, or assignment, under federal, national, or state/provincial bankruptcy laws or any federal, national, or state/provincial insolvency law has been filed by or against, or a receiver, fiscal agent, or similar officer having been appointed by a court for the business or property of (any one of the foregoing herein referred to as a "Bankruptcy Filing"), such individual Person (whom at or about the time of such Bankruptcy Filing, was a Tour Operator Member or was engaged in a business as a Tour Operator, or any Person (whom at or about the time of such Bankruptcy Filing, was a Tour Operator Member or was engaged in business as a Tour Operator) in which the individual Person was a general partner, principal executive officer, director, or 10% or more partner, member, shareholder or equity participant in a business, at or within six (6) months before the time of such Bankruptcy Filing, and (ii) such Bankruptcy Filing has resulted in a loss, which has not been satisfied in full, or for which acceptable arrangements for the satisfaction of such loss in full, have not been made, to the NTA, NTACPP Trust and/or any NTA Member; or

B. Whom, within the past five (5) years immediately preceding the NTA Convention and/or NTA Spring Meet, has been convicted of a felony or for whom at the time of the NTA Convention and/or NTA Spring Meet is the subject of a pending criminal felony (as interpreted under Kentucky law) proceeding.

The NTA shall be authorized to exclude any such

individual Person from attendance at any NTA Convention and/or NTA Spring Meet, with or without notice to the NTA Member, whom such individual Person is associated. A NTA Member who has had an individual Person, whom that NTA Member designated as its/his/her representative, excluded from attendance at a NTA Convention and/or NTA Spring Meet may within thirty (30) days of notice of such exclusion, file with the NTA Staff, a request for reconsideration of such exclusion, stating the reason why reconsideration is justified. Upon receipt of a properly filed request for reconsideration, NTA Staff shall submit such request for reconsideration to the Board of Directors, which shall act upon such request within thirty (30) days after the date the request is received by the NTA Staff. During the pendency of such request for reconsideration, the individual Person subject to being excluded from attendance at a NTA Convention and/or NTA Spring Meet shall not be subject to exclusion from such event(s). The affirmative vote of not less than two-thirds (2/3) of the entire Board of Directors shall be required to set aside the exclusion of an individual Person from attendance at a NTA Convention and/or NTA Spring Meet. The Board of Directors' written decision upon such request shall be final, unappealable and binding upon such NTA Member. If there is a substantive change in the basis for exclusion of an individual Person from attendance at a NTA Convention and/or NTA Spring Meet, the involved NTA Member may resubmit his/her/its request for reconsideration, according to the procedures provided by the Board of Directors from time to time.

11.0 Definitions

For the purposes hereof:

A. The term "Affiliate" shall mean a Person, other than an individual person, which is a separate legal entity, in which Fifty Percent (50%) or more of the equity interest is owned directly or indirectly by another Person.

B. The term "North America" and "North American" shall mean the United States and its territorial properties, Canada and its territorial properties and Mexico.

C. The term "Packaged Travel" shall mean a package and combination of two or more types of travel components (i.e., transportation, lodging, meals, attractions, escort and guide services) not owned, managed or controlled by the Tour Operator into and as a product, which is produced, assembled, promoted and sold as a package for an all inclusive price.

D. The term "Receptive Packaged Travel" shall mean a package and combination of two or more types of travel components (i.e., transportation, lodging, meals, attractions, escort and guide services) not owned, managed or controlled by the Receptive Tour Operator into and as a product, which is produced, assembled, promoted and sold as a package for an all inclusive price to a Tour Operator, for use by the Tour Operator, as a part of the Tour Operators Packaged Travel product.

E. The term "Person" shall mean any sole proprietorship, partnership, firm, trust, limited liability company, estate, corporation, unincorporated organization or association or local, state or federal governmental regulatory authority or agency.

F. The term "Separate Legal Entity" shall mean a Person, capable of conducting a business and recognized by applicable law as a separate and distinct legal entity.

7

Global Tourism, Tourist Traffic and Tourist Boards Act

THE MALDIVES TOURISM ACT (1999)

An Unofficial Translation of the Act

1. (a) This Act provides for the determination of zones and islands for the development of tourism in the Maldives; the leasing of islands for development as tourist resorts, the leasing of land for development as tourist hotels and tourist guesthouses, the leasing of places for development as marinas, the management of all such facilities; and the operation of tourist vessels, diving centres and travel agencies, and the regulation of persons providing such services.

(b) This Act shall be cited as the "Maldives Tourism Act".

2. The leasing of islands and land for development as tourist resorts and tourist hotels, the leasing of places for development as marinas, the management of tourist resorts, tourist hotels, establishments such as tourist guesthouses and marinas; and the operation of tourist vessels, shall all be in accordance with this Act and regulations made under it.

3. The management of diving centres and travel agencies and the provision of their services in the Maldives shall be in accordance with regulations made under this Act.

4. Zones for the development of tourism in the Maldives, islands for development as tourist resorts and places for development as marinas shall be determined by the President.

On Tourist Resorts

5. Islands and land for development as tourist resorts shall be leased to the party that submits the best-qualified bid in respect of such islands or land in accordance with pre-established procedures in a public tender held by the Ministry of Tourism. Islands or land in which the Government makes an investment wholly or in joint venture shall be exempted from the procedure provided herein.

6. A tourist resort on an island or land leased under this Act shall be developed under a [lease] agreement to be entered into between the Government and the lessee of such island or land. This [lease] agreement shall contain the following:-

(a) [the name of] the island or land being leased;
(b) the period of the lease;
(c) where a specific time period is granted for construction [of the tourist resort] during the term of the lease, such period and commencement date of the operation of the [tourist] resort;
(d) circumstances warranting premature termination of the agreement and the procedures to be followed upon such circumstances arising;
(e) the amount of the lease rent, method of its assessment and the manner of its payment;
(f) the procedures to be followed in the event of a

sublease of the [tourist] resort or the transfer of management of the resort to a third party; and

(g) the procedures to be followed in the event of a breach of the agreement by the lessee.

7. (a) An island or land for development as a tourist resort shall be leased subject to .,the condition that such island or land shall, upon expiration of the period specified in' the lease agreement or upon premature annulment of the agreement, be returned to the Government in the same condition as it existed when the resort was under operation, in order for the Government to act in accordance with subsection (b) of this section.

(b) Upon expiration of the lease period of an island or land for development as a tourist resort or upon annulment of the agreement prior to the expiration of its term other than either at the request of the lessee or on breach of the agreement by the lessee, and upon return of the island or land to the Government, the monetary value of the buildings and items on the island or land, after an assessment has been made in accordance with principles determined by the Auditor General of the Maldives and after deducting an amount for depreciation until the date of return of the island or land to the Government, shall be paid by the Government to the former lessee within two years from the date of the return of that island or land.

(c) Where an island or land returned to the Government in the circumstances specified in subsection (b) of this section either upon expiration of the lease period or upon annulment of the [lease] agreement prior to the expiration of its term, is leased under section 11 of this Act to the former lessee of the island or land, the monetary value in respect of the buildings and items on the island or land as provided in subsection (b) of this section shall not be payable to that lessee.

8. Save for islands and land leased for development as tourist resorts as provided in section 9 of this Act, islands or land for development as tourist resorts shall be leased for a maximum period of 25 years from the date possession of the island or land is granted to the lessee.

9. (a) Where the initial investment made for the development of a tourist resort on an island or land exceeds US$ 10 million, the Government may in its discretion grant a lease of the island or land for a maximum period of 35 years after due consideration is made of the size of the investment and the standard of the proposed resort.

(b) Where the lessee of an island or land for development of a tourist resort is a public company that meets all of the conditions specified below, such island or land may be leased for a period of 50 years:-

(i) the [public] company is registered in the Maldives;

(ii) the development and operation of tourist resorts is included as an object in the memorandum of association of the [public] company:

(iii) the [public] company's shareholders are all Maldivian citizens and at least 50'."o of the companies shares are sold to the public;

(iv) no more than 1% of the publicly-held shares are held shares are held by a single shareholder except where the shareholder is an investment company, in which case no more than 5% of the publicly-held shares should be held by that investment company; and the shares were sold to the public in a manner feasible for members of the public to purchase them and the shares were not sold to a determinate group of persons.

10. (a) Upon the coming into force of this Act, an additional 4 years shall: be granted to the lease period of an island or land leased for development as a tourist resort prior to the coming into force of this Act.

(b) An additional 25 years shall be granted to the lease period of an island or land leased for development as a tourist resort upon application for such extension provided that the lessee has registered as a public company, has sold at least 50% of its shares to the public and satisfies the conditions specified in subsection 9(b) of this Act, and provided further that the application for the extension of the lease period v as made within 4 years from the date of the coming into force of this Act or within 4 years from the date possession of the island or land was granted in the case of a lessee to whom an island or land was leased after the coming into force of this Act.

(c) If a lessee of an island or land leased for development as a tourist resort has registered as a public company, has sold at least 50% of its shares to the public and has made an application for an extension of the lease period in respect of such island or land, then, provided such company satisfies the conditions set forth in subsection 9(b) of this Act, an additional 20 years shall be granted to the lease period of such island or land where the application was made after a lapse of 4 years from the commencement of the lease period but before the expiration of half of the term of the lease period, and if the application is made at any time after the expiration of half of the term of the lease period, then an additional period equivalent to the term of the remaining lease period shall be granted to the lease period.

11. (a) Upon expiration of the term of the lease agreement of an island or land leased for development as a tourist resort or upon expiration of the period extended under section 10 of this Act or where the lessee is divested of possession of the island or land due to annulment of the agreement prior to the expiration of the lease period, then a fresh lease in respect of such island or land may be made in accordance with the manner provided in section 5 of this Act and for a period specified in this Act.

(b) Parties wishing to lease an island or land placed in public tender to be leased afresh in accordance with subsection (a) of this section shall when submitting their bid undertake that in the event the lease is granted to such party, they will pay to the Government the monetary value of the buildings and items on the island as assessed in accordance with the principles determined by the Auditor General of the Maldives after an amount has been deducted for depreciation, within 1 year from the date possession of the island or land is granted to such party; provided, however, that where the former lessee of such an island or land submits a bid to lease the island or land afresh, such a lessee shall not be required to undertake to pay the monetary value of the [buildings and] items on the island.

12. An investment made on an island or land leased by the Government for development as a tourist resort may be sold or the leasehold rights accruing to a lessee under an agreement made between the Government and the lessee may be sold or transferred or the shares of a lessee of an

island or land that is a company may be transferred upon obtaining written approval from the Ministry of Tourism and in accordance with any conditions stipulated by that Ministry. The transfer of shares of public companies is excluded from this provision.

13. Where the lessee is a public company that has the lease of an island or land for a period of 50 years under section 9(b) of this Act or for a period extended under section 10, and either converts to a private company or fails to satisfy any of the conditions specified in section 9(b) of this Act, then the period of extension of the lease granted to such company by reason of being a public company shall be deducted.

14. (a) Where an island or land leased under this Act for development as a tourist resort is required for defence of the Maldives, possession of such island or land may be divested from the lessee without any prior notice being given to that effect. Save as provided herein, the possession of an island or land may be divested from the lessee prior to the expiration of the lease only in accordance with the provisions of the [lease] agreement of such island or land.

(b) Where possession of an island or land leased for development as a tourist resort is divested pursuant to sub-section (a) of this section on the grounds of it being required for defence of the Maldives, equitable compensation shall be paid in respect of the investment made on such island or land.

15. (a) Felling of coconut palms and trees on an island or land leased for development as a tourist resort, dredging of the lagoon of such an island, reclamation of land, or any other' activity determined by the Ministry of Tourism as may be likely to cause a permanent change to the [natural] environment of such places, may only be carried out after obtaining written permission from that Ministry and in accordance with relevant regulations made by it.

(b) Any application pursuant to subsection (a) of this section for permission of the Ministry of Tourism to carry out dredging of the lagoon of an island or reclamation of land or any other activity that may cause a permanent change to the [natural] environment of such a place shall contain the following:–

(1) evidence that the proposed change is fundamental for the provision of services from such a place; and

(2) an environmental impact assessment report submitted to and approved by the Ministry of Home Affairs, Housing and Environment.

16. (a) Every resort developed on an island or land leased in accordance with section 5 of this Act shall be operated after registering the same at the Ministry of Tourism and after obtaining a licence issued by the Ministry of Tourism to operate a tourist resort.

(b) licence to operate a tourist resort shall be issued in respect of establishments that satisfy the following conditions:-

(1) the construction [of the tourist resorl] is completed in accordance with guidelines determined by the Ministry of Tourism; and

(2) the services determined by the Ministry of Tourism to be necessary at such establishments are made available at the tourist resort.

On Tourist Hotels and Tourist Guesthouses

17. Neither a tourist hotel nor a tourist guesthouse shall be operated in the Maldives except after registering the same at the Ministry of Tourism and after obtaining a licence issued by the Ministry to operate such establishments.

18. A licence to operate a tourist hotel or a tourist guesthouse shall be issued to those establishments that satisfy the following conditions:-

(a) the building and facilities are in accordance with guidelines made by the Ministry of Tourism;

(b) the services determined by the Ministry of Tourism to be necessary at such an establishment are made available at the tourist hotel or tourist guesthouse;

(c) the registration fee prescribed in section 21 of this Act is paid; and

(d) the establishment is situated on an island determined pursuant to section 4 of this Act for the development of tourism.

19. Where the Government leases any land for development as a tourist hotel or a tourist guesthouse, such a lease shall be made in accordance with the provisions of this Act relating to the leasing of islands or land for development as tourist resorts. Furthermore, the provisions of this Act relating to tourist resorts shall also apply [equally] in respect of tourist hotels and tourist guesthouses.

20. No tourist shall be provided accommodation for payment in any establishment other than a tourist hotel or tourist guesthouse registered and licensed under this Act or a tourist resort or tourist vessel licensed under this Act.

21. Every tourist hotel or tourist guesthouse shall he registered upon payment of a registration fee of MRf 10,000 in the case of a tourist hotel and MRf 5,000 in the case of a tourist guesthouse.

On Tourist Vessels

22. No tourist vessel shall be operated in the Maldives except after obtaining a licence from the Ministry of Tourism to operate such a vessel.

23. A licence for the operation of a tourist vessel shall be issued to vessels that satisfy the following conditions:-

(a) the vessel and its facilities comply with guidelines determined by the Ministry of Tourism;

(b) the services determined by the Ministry of Tourism to be necessary on such vessel are made available on the vessel; and

(c) the vessel is duly registered at the Ministry of Transport and Civil Aviation.

24. (a) No foreign-registered tourist vessel arriving in the Maldives shall travel or anchor within any of the territorial waters of the Maldives except after obtaining permission from the relevant Government authorities and from the Ministry of Tourism in accordance with its determined regulations.

(b) The permission referred to in sub-section (a) of this section for travelling and anchoring in the Maldives shall be issued by the Ministry of Tourism upon payment of a fee of MRf 5,000. The [foreign-registered tourist] vessel's local agent in the Maldives shall be liable for the payment of this fee.

On Marinas

25. Marinas shall be developed and operated in the Maldives at such places leased pursuant to section 26 of this Act.

26. Places for development as marinas shall he leased in accordance with the provisions of this Act relating to the leasing of islands and land for development as tourist resorts. Furthermore, the provisions of this Act relating to tourist resorts shall also apply [equally] in respect of marinas.

27. Marinas shall be developed and operated after obtaining a licence issued by the Ministry of Tourism to

operate such places and in compliance with guidelines determined by that Ministry in relation to the development and operation of marinas.

28. The licence referred to in section 27 of this Act for the operation of marinas shall be issued in respect of marinas that satisfy the following conditions:-

(a) [the marina] is built in compliance with the guidelines determined by the Ministry of Tourism and is in possession of the required permission from the relevant Government authorities; and
(b) the services determined by the Ministry of Tourism to be necessary at such place are made available from the marina.

On Diving Centres

29. No diving centre providing services to tourists shall be operated in the Maldives except after registering the same at the Ministry of Tourism and after obtaining a licence [to do so] issued by that Ministry.

30. The licence referred to in section 29 of this Act for the operation of a diving centre shall be issued to parties that satisfy the following conditions:-

(a) where the party is a company or other business organisation, the operation of diving centres is included as an object in the memorandum of association of that company or business organisation;
(b) where the party is a foreign company or business organisation, it is registered at the Ministry of Trade and Industries as a company or business organisation carrying on business in the Maldives;
(c) the [physical] presence of a diving centre operated in accordance with the guidelines provided in the regulations made under this Act, and the services

determined by the Ministry of Tourism to be necessary at such centre are made available at the diving centre; and

(d) the registration fee prescribed in section 31 of this Act is paid.

31. A diving centre referred to in section 29 of this Act shall he registered upon payment of a registration fee of MRf 5,000.

On Travel Agents

32. No person shall provide travel agency services in the Maldives except after obtaining a licence [to do so] issued by the Ministry of Tourism.

33. A licence to provide travel agency services shall be issued to parties that satisfy the following conditions:–

(a) where the party is a company or other business organisation, the provision of travel agency services is included as an object in the memorandum of association of that company or business organisation;

(b) where the party is a foreign company or business organisation, it is registered at the Ministry of Trade and Industries as a company or business organisation carrying on business in the Maldives: and

(c) the [physical] presence of an office operated in compliance with guidelines provided in regulations made under this Act, and the services determined by the Ministry of Tourism to be necessary at such office are made available from the travel agency.

34. (a) No person shall act as a tour guide in the Maldives except after obtaining permission from the Ministry of Tourism in accordance with regulations made by that Ministry.

(b) Every person acting as a tour guide shall, whilst acting in the course of business as a tour guide, attach to his attire in a manner identifiable to others the permission issued to him.

Tax

35. (a) The sum of US$6, or its equivalent in a foreign currency acceptable to the Maldives Monetary Authority, shall be collected as tax payable to the Government of the Maldives from each tourist per day of stay at a tourist resort, tourist hotel, tourist guesthouse or tourist vessel. The management of the establishment where the tourist was provided accommodation shall be liable for collection of that tax from tourists and payment of the due amount to the Government. The amount of tax due in respect of the preceding month shall be paid by the 15th day of the current month.

(b) The tax referred to in subsection (a) of this section shal1 be collected for each day of stay in the Maldives from every tourist that is on board every tourist vessel which has been granted permission under section 24 of this Act, except for those vessels referred to in subsection (c) of this section. The tax shall be paid to the Government prior to the departure of the tourist vessel from the Maldives. The liability as regards payment of the tax shall be borne by the tourist vessel's local agent.

(c) Any foreign-registered tourist vessel arriving in the Maldives and staying within its territorial waters for a period not exceeding 24 hours shall not be required to pay the tax referred to in subsection (a) and (b) of this section.

36. Information regarding tourists that were resident in the tourist resort, tourist hotel, tourist guesthouse or

tourist vessel during the preceding month shall be submitted to the Department of Inland Revenue before the 8th day of the current month. Such information shall be submitted in accordance with regulations made by that Department and in a format as may be determined by it.

37. (a) Where the management of a tourist resort, tourist hotel or tourist guesthouse or the operator of a tourist vessel is in violation of this Act as regards payment of tax due, a fine of MRf 1,000 per bed registered at such establishment or vessel at the time of such violation shall be paid to the Department of Inland Revenue in addition to the payment of overdue tax.

(b) The tax referred to in section 35 of this Act and the fine referred to in subsection (a) of this section shall be paid by the end of the current month. In the event of default in payment during that period, the licence issued to operate such an establishment shall be revoked.

(c) Where a licence is revoked under sub-section (b) of this section, it shall be re-issued upon settlement of the defaulted payment of tax and fine.

38. Guests of the Government that are accorded special immunities and privileges shall be exempted from the collection of tax specified in this Act.

Miscellaneous Matters

39. No foreign party shall engage in any tourism related activity referred to in this Act in the Maldives except after entering into the agreement specified in Act No. 25/79 (Maldives Foreign Investments Act) and after registering the investment at the Ministry of Tourism in accordance with the provisions

40. The President shall have the discretion to; determine the principles for exemption of import duties on materials

imported for the construction of tourist resorts or tourist hotels situated on land leased for the development of such under this Act. the construction of marinas or for the purposes of the upgradation of such establishments, and to exempt such duty in accordance with those principles.

41. All parties engaged in tourism related activities shall, in accordance with regulations stipulated by the Ministry of Tourism. provide it with information required to prepare the tourism statistics of the Maldives.

42. Licences for the operation of tourist resorts, tourist hotels, tourist guesthouses, marinas. tourist vessels, diving centres and travel agencies shall be issued under this Act for a period of 5 years. All other licences shall be issued for the period stated in regulations made by the Ministry of Tourism. Licences shall be renewed upon expiration of the period for which they have been issued.

43. All licenses issued under this Act shall, unless otherwise provided in this Act, be displayed in a prominent manner in the establishment to which the license was issued.

44. The Ministry of Tourism shall have the discretion to classify tourist resorts, tourist hotels, tourist guesthouses and tourist vessels into various classes and to determine the services and standards of those services to be provided by such establishments based upon their classifications.

45. The Ministry of Tourism shall have the discretion to monitor tourist resorts, tourist hotels, tourist guesthouses, tourist vessels, marinas, diving centres and travel agencies and to ensure that the services provided by such establishments are in accordance with guidelines determined by the Ministry of Tourism, the provisions of this Act and any regulations made under it.

46. Where the standard of service provided by a tourist

resort, tourist hotel, tourist guesthouse, tourist vessel, marina, diving centre or travel agency falls below the guidelines determined by the Ministry of Tourism, then the Ministry may in its discretion impose upon such establishment a fine not exceeding MRf 1,000,000 and, taking into account the extent of the default, suspend the license issued to the establishment until the default is rectified.

47. Except where it is otherwise stated in any other provision of this Act, a party in default of a provision of this Act shall be fined by an amount not exceeding MRf 100,000.

48. Those establishments specified in this Act as being required to be registered or licensed but which are not either registered or licensed prior to the coming into force of this Act, shall be registered or licensed within 1 year of the date of the coming into force of this Act.

49. Any regulations that are required to be made under this Act, unless specified otherwise, shall be made and enforced by a party determined by the President for such purpose.

50. In this Act, unless the context otherwise requires: –

(a) "tourist resort" means an island or a designated area of an island that has been developed to accommodate tourists and to provide board and lodging facilities for them;

(b) "tourist hotel" means an establishment, other than a tourist resort or tourist guesthouse, that has been developed to provide board and lodging or [only] lodging for tourists for a payment decided at a certain rate per day of stay;

(c) "tourist guesthouse" means an establishment, other than a tourist resort or a tourist hotel, that has been developed, in compliance with standards determined by the Ministry of Tourism, to provide board and lodging or[only] lodging for tourists for a payment decided at a certain rate per day of stay;

(d) "tourist vessel" means a seagoing vessel that has been developed, in compliance with standards determined by the Ministry of Tourism, to provide board and lodging for tourists for a payment decided at a certain rate per day of stay on board such vessel;

(e) "marina" means harbours developed for anchoring yachts and such vessels and to provide various services to those vessels;

(f) "diving centres" mean diving schools, diving bases and all other parties that provide diving services for tourists;

(g) "travel agency service" means services provided by travel agents, tour operators and other parties engaged in arranging travel on a commercial basis for persons travelling to or from the Republic of Maldives and excludes those organising Hajj and Umra [pilgrimages] for Maldivian citizens;

(h) "investment company" means banks, insurance companies and such financial companies and institutions formed to manage and invest funds of various persons; and

(i) "tourist" means every person that enters the Maldives who is not a Maldivian citizen and is not in possession of a "resident permit". A "resident permit" is a permit issued pursuant to regulations of the relevant authorities permitting an individual to be resident in the Maldives whilst not being a tourist.

51. Upon the coming into force of this Act. Act No. 15/79 (Law on Tourism in the Maldives) and Act No. 3/94 (Law on Leasing of Uninhabited Islands for the Development of Tourist Resorts) shall be repealed.

TOURISM AUSTRALIA ACT (2004)

No. 74, 2004

The Parliament of Australia enacts:

PART 1: PRELIMINARY

1. Short title

This Act may be cited as the *Tourism Australia Act 2004*.

2. Commencement

(1) Each provision of this Act specified in column 1 of the table commences, or is taken to have commenced, in accordance with column 2 of the table. Any other statement in column 2 has effect according to its terms.

Commencement information

Column 1	Column 2	Column 3
Provision(s)	**Commencement**	**Date/Details**
1. Sections 1 and 2 and anything in this Act not elsewhere covered by this table	The day on which this Act receives the Royal Assent.	23 June 2004
2. Sections 3 to 64	A single day to be fixed by Proclamation. However, if any of the provision(s) do not commence	1 July 2004 (s 2(1); *Gazette* 2004, GN26)

within the period of 6 months
beginning on the day on
which this Act receives the
Royal Assent, they
commence on the first
day after the end of
that period.

Note: This table relates only to the provisions of this Act as originally passed by the Parliament and assented to. It will not be expanded to deal with provisions inserted in this Act after assent.

(2) Column 3 of the table contains additional information that is not part of this Act. Information in this column may be added to or edited in any published version of this Act.

3. Definitions

In this Act, unless the contrary intention appears:

appointed member means a member other than the Managing Director.

Australia, when used in a geographical sense, includes the external Territories.

Board means the Board of Directors of Tourism Australia.

Chair means the Chair of the Board.

Deputy Chair means the Deputy Chair of the Board.

government member means the government member of the Board.

Managing Director means the Managing Director of Tourism Australia.

member means a member of the Board (including the Chair and Deputy Chair).

4. Extended Geographical Application of this Act

(1) This Act extends to every external Territory.

(2) This Act applies both within and outside Australia.

PART 2: TOURISM AUSTRALIA

5. Establishment

(1) Tourism Australia is established by this section.

(2) Tourism Australia:

(a) is a body corporate; and

(b) must have a seal; and

(c) may sue and be sued.

Note: The *Commonwealth Authorities and Companies Act 1997* applies to Tourism Australia. That Act deals with matters relating to Commonwealth authorities, including reporting and accountability, banking and investment, and conduct of executive officers.

(3) The seal of Tourism Australia is to be kept in such custody as the Board directs, and is not to be used except as authorised by the Board.

(4) All courts, judges and persons acting judicially must:

(a) take judicial notice of the imprint of the seal of Tourism Australia appearing on a document; and

(b) presume that the document was duly sealed.

6. Objects

Tourism Australia's objects are:

(a) to influence people to travel to Australia, including for events; and

(b) to influence people travelling to Australia to also travel throughout Australia; and

(c) to influence Australians to travel throughout Australia, including for events; and

(d) to help foster a sustainable tourism industry in Australia; and

(e) to help increase the economic benefits to Australia from tourism.

7. Functions

(1) Tourism Australia's functions are:

(a) to increase the awareness of potential international travellers of Australia as a destination; and

(b) to increase the awareness of potential domestic travellers of Australia as a place to travel; and

(c) to increase the knowledge of potential travellers, both international and domestic, of Australia; and

(d) to increase the desire of potential international travellers to travel to Australia; and

(e) to increase the desire of potential travellers, both international and domestic, to travel throughout Australia; and

(f) to conduct research into, and analysis of, international and domestic travel; and

(g) to report on trends in international and domestic travel; and

(h) to communicate effectively with the Australian tourism industry on issues that may affect it; and

(i) to increase awareness throughout Australia of the contribution of tourism to Australia's economy, society and environment.

(2) In performing its functions, Tourism Australia must

have regard to the needs of the Australian tourism industry and government.

(3) Tourism Australia may perform its functions:

(a) in cooperation with the tourism industry; and

(b) in cooperation with Australian governments and agencies, and foreign governments.

(4) Tourism Australia may perform its functions to the extent only that they are not in excess of the functions that may be conferred on it by virtue of any of the legislative powers of the Parliament, and, in particular, may perform its functions:

(a) for purposes related to external affairs; and

(b) in the course of, or in relation to, trade and commerce with other countries, among the States, between Territories or between a Territory and a State; and

(c) for purposes related to a Territory; and

(d) by means of a communication using a postal, telegraphic, telephonic or other like service within the meaning of paragraph 51(v) of the Constitution; and

(e) for purposes related to the collection, compilation, analysis, use and dissemination of statistics; and

(f) for purposes related to a corporation to which paragraph 51(xx) of the Constitution applies; and

(g) for purposes related to lighthouses, lightships, beacons and buoys; and

(h) for purposes related to matters incidental to the execution of any of the legislative powers of the Parliament or the executive power of the Commonwealth; and

(i) for purposes related to a Commonwealth place

within the meaning of the *Commonwealth Places (Application of Laws) Act 1970*; and

(j) for purposes related to the executive power of the Commonwealth; and

(k) for purposes related to money appropriated for the purposes of the Commonwealth; and

(l) for purposes related to the granting of financial assistance to a State on such terms and conditions as the Parliament thinks fit; and

(m) in so far as it is appropriate for those functions to be performed by Tourism Australia on behalf of the Government of the Commonwealth as the national Government of Australia; and

(n) for purposes for which it is appropriate for the Parliament as the national Parliament of Australia to authorise Tourism Australia to perform functions; and

(o) by way of providing a service, if the provision of the service utilises Tourism Australia's spare capacity and does not impede Tourism Australia's capacity to perform its other functions.

8. Powers

(1) Subject to subsection (3), Tourism Australia has power to do all things necessary or convenient to be done for or in connection with the performance of its functions.

(2) Tourism Australia's powers include, but are not limited to, the following powers:

(a) to enter into contracts, agreements or arrangements; and

(b) to establish offices; and

(c) to acquire, hold and dispose of real and personal property; and

(d) to lease the whole or any part of any land or building; and

(e) to occupy, use and control any land or building owned, or held under lease, by the Commonwealth and made available to Tourism Australia; and

(f) to arrange for the manufacture, and distribution (whether by sale or otherwise) of anything bearing a mark, symbol or writing associated with Tourism Australia; and

(g) to accept gifts, grants, bequests and devises made to it; and

(h) to act as trustee of money and other property vested in it on trust; and

(i) to enter into cooperative arrangements with other persons; and

(j) to appoint agents and attorneys, and act as an agent for other persons; and

(k) to obtain commercial sponsorship; and

(l) to charge for work done, services provided, and products and information supplied, by or on behalf of Tourism Australia; and

(m) to provide financial assistance; and

(n) to do such other things as it is authorised to do by or under this Act; and

(o) to do anything incidental to any of its powers.

(3) Tourism Australia must not carry on business as a travel agent.

PART 3: THE BOARD OF DIRECTORS OF TOURISM AUSTRALIA

Division 1: The Board

9. Establishment

The Board of Directors of Tourism Australia is established by this section.

10. Functions

The Board has the following functions:

(a) to ensure the proper and efficient performance of Tourism Australia's functions;

(b) to determine Tourism Australia's policy in relation to any matter.

11. Powers

The Board has power to do all things necessary or convenient to be done for or in connection with the performance of its functions.

12. Membership

The Board consists of the following members:

(a) the Chair;

(b) the Deputy Chair;

(c) the government member;

(d) the Managing Director;

(e) 6 other members.

Note: Section 18B of the *Acts Interpretation Act 1901* deals with the title of the Chair.

13. Appointing members

(1) The members of the Board (except the Managing Director) are to be appointed by the Minister by written instrument.

(2) The appointment of a member is not invalid because of a defect or irregularity in connection with the appointment.

14. Qualifications for appointment

(1) The Minister may appoint a person as a member (other than the government member) only if the

Minister is satisfied that the person has high level expertise in one or more of the following areas:

(a) international tourism;
(b) domestic tourism;
(c) corporate governance;
(d) financial management;
(e) marketing and promotion;
(f) business;
(g) investment strategies;
(h) infrastructure in Australia that supports tourism, including events;
(i) transport networks;
(j) economic analysis;
(k) current and emerging technologies;
(l) regional development;
(m) environmental management;
(n) Australian indigenous tourism or culture.

(2) The government member is to be a person appointed or engaged under the *Public Service Act 1999*.

(3) The Minister may appoint a person as government member only if the Minister is satisfied that the person has expertise in:

(a) the formulation of government policy; and
(b) public administration.

15. Term and basis of appointment

(1) An appointed member (other than the government member) holds office for the period specified in the instrument of appointment. The period must not exceed 3 years.

(2) A person appointed as government member holds office for the period specified in the instrument of appointment.

(3) An appointed member holds office on a part-time basis.

16. Acting appointments

(1) The Deputy Chair is to act as the Chair:

(a) during a vacancy in the office of Chair (whether or not an appointment has previously been made to the office); or

(b) during any period, or during all periods, when the Chair is absent from duty or from Australia, or is, for any reason, unable to perform the duties of the office.

Note: Under section 33A of the *Acts Interpretation Act 1901*, this Act applies in relation to a person acting in a particular office as if the person were the holder of the office.

(2) The Minister may appoint an appointed member (other than the government member) to act as the Deputy Chair:

(a) during a vacancy in the office of Deputy Chair (whether or not an appointment has previously been made to the office); or

(b) during any period, or during all periods, when the Deputy Chair is acting as the Chair, or is, for any reason, unable to attend meetings of the Board.

(3) The Minister may appoint a person to act as an appointed member (other than as Chair or Deputy Chair):

(a) during a vacancy in the office of an appointed member (whether or not an appointment has previously been made to the office); or

(b) during any period, or during all periods, when a member is acting as the Deputy Chair, or is, for any reason, unable to attend meetings of the Board.

(4) Anything done by or in relation to a person purporting to act under this section is not invalid merely because:

(a) the occasion for the appointment had not arisen; or

(b) there was a defect or irregularity in connection with the appointment; or

(c) the appointment had ceased to have effect; or

(d) the occasion to act had not arisen or had ceased.

17. Members' remuneration and allowances

(1) An appointed member is to be paid the remuneration that is determined by the Remuneration Tribunal. If no determination of that remuneration by the Tribunal is in operation, the appointed member is to be paid the remuneration that is prescribed.

(2) An appointed member is to be paid the allowances that are prescribed.

(3) This section has effect subject to the *Remuneration Tribunal Act 1973*.

18. Leave of absence

(1) The Minister may grant leave of absence to the Chair on the terms and conditions that the Minister determines.

(2) The Chair may grant leave of absence to any other appointed member on the terms and conditions that the Chair determines.

19. Resignation

An appointed member may resign his or her appointment by giving the Minister a written resignation.

20. Termination of appointment

(1) The Minister may at any time, in writing, terminate the appointment of the government member.

(2) The Minister may terminate the appointment of an appointed member (other than the government member) for misbehaviour or physical or mental incapacity.

(3) The Minister must terminate the appointment of an appointed member (other than the government member) if:

(a) the appointed member:

(i) becomes bankrupt; or

(ii) applies to take the benefit of any law for the relief of bankrupt or insolvent debtors; or

(iii) compounds with his or her creditors; or

(iv) makes an assignment of his or her remuneration for the benefit of his or her creditors; or

(b) the appointed member is absent, except on leave of absence, from 3 consecutive meetings of the Board; or

(c) the appointed member fails, without reasonable excuse, to comply with Subdivision B of Division 4 of Part 3 of the *Commonwealth Authorities and Companies Act 1997.*

21. Other terms and conditions

An appointed member holds office on the terms and conditions (if any) in relation to matters not covered by this Act that are determined by the Minister in writing.

Division 2: Board procedures

22. Convening meetings

(1) The Board must hold the meetings that are necessary for the efficient performance of its role.

(2) Meetings are to be held at the times and places that the Board determines.

(3) The Chair:

(a) may convene a meeting; and

(b) must convene a meeting if requested in writing by 3 or more other members.

(4) The Minister may, at any time, convene a meeting of the Board.

23. Presiding at meetings

(1) The Chair must preside at all meetings at which he or she is present.

(2) If the Chair is not present at a meeting but the Deputy Chair is present, the Deputy Chair must preside.

(3) If neither the Chair nor the Deputy Chair is present at a meeting, the other members present must appoint one of their number (other than the Managing Director or the government member) to preside.

24. Quorum

(1) At a meeting of the Board a quorum is constituted by 5 members.

(2) However, if:

(a) a member is required by section 27J of the *Commonwealth Authorities and Companies Act 1997* not to be present during the deliberations, or to take part in any decision, of the Board with respect to a particular matter; and

(b) when the member leaves the meeting concerned there is no longer a quorum present; those remaining members constitute a quorum for the purpose of any deliberation or decision at that meeting with respect to that matter.

25. Voting at meetings

(1) A question arising at a meeting is to be determined by a majority of the votes of the members present and voting.

(2) The person presiding at a meeting has:

(a) a deliberative vote; and

(b) if necessary, also a casting vote.

Note: Subdivision B of Division 4 of Part 3 of the *Commonwealth Authorities and Companies Act 1997* has rules for "directors" about disclosing, and voting on matters involving, material personal interests.

26. Resolutions

(1) The Board may pass a resolution without a Board meeting being held if all the members entitled to vote on the resolution sign a document containing a statement that they are in favour of the resolution set out in the document.

(2) Separate copies of a document may be used for signing by the members if the wording of the resolution and statement is identical in each copy.

(3) The resolution is passed when the last of the members signs.

27. Other procedural matters

(1) Subject to this Part, the Board may regulate the conduct of proceedings at its meetings as it thinks fit.

Note: Section 33B of the *Acts Interpretation Act 1901* contains further information about the ways in which members may participate in meetings.

(2) The Board must:

(a) keep minutes of its meetings; and

(b) keep a record of resolutions passed in accordance with section 26.

Division 3: Advisory panels

28. Advisory panels

(1) The Board may, in writing, establish advisory panels to assist with the performance of Tourism Australia's functions.

Note 1: The Board may, for example, establish advisory panels to assist with the performance of Tourism Australia's functions in relation to international tourism, domestic tourism, events and research.

Note 2: Subsection 33(3) of the *Acts Interpretation Act 1901* provides for the repeal, variation etc. of instruments.

(2) An advisory panel consists of such persons as the Board appoints to the panel in writing.

Note: Subsection 33(3) of the *Acts Interpretation Act 1901* provides for the repeal, variation etc. of instruments.

(3) The office of member of an advisory panel is not a public office within the meaning of the *Remuneration Tribunal Act 1973*.

29. Procedures of advisory panels etc.

An advisory panel may determine the way in which it is to carry out its task (including when and where it meets and procedures to be followed in relation to its meetings).

30. Disclosure of interests at meetings

(1) A member of an advisory panel who has a direct or

indirect pecuniary interest in a matter being considered or about to be considered by the panel must disclose the nature of the interest at a meeting of the panel as soon as possible after the relevant facts have come to the member's knowledge.

(2) A disclosure under subsection (1) must be recorded in the minutes of the meeting of the panel.

(3) The Board must terminate the appointment of a member of an advisory panel if the member fails, without reasonable excuse, to comply with subsection (1).

31. Resignation

A member of an advisory panel may resign by giving the Board a written resignation.

32. Other terms and conditions

A member of an advisory panel holds office on such terms and conditions (if any) in respect of matters not provided for by this Act as are determined by the Board in writing with the Minister's written approval.

PART 4: CORPORATE PLANNING AND ACCOUNTABILITY

Division 1: Corporate plan and annual operational plan

33. Corporate plan

(1) The Board must prepare a corporate plan for Tourism Australia by 1 May each financial year (or by such later day as the Minister in a particular financial year allows).

(2) The first corporate plan must be prepared as soon as practicable after the commencement of this section.

(3) A corporate plan must be for a period of 3 financial years.

(4) In preparing a plan, the Board must consult:

(a) State and Territory tourism authorities; and

(b) anyone else concerned with tourism that the Board considers appropriate; and

(c) anyone else specified by the Minister in writing.

(5) The Board may revise the corporate plan on its own initiative at any other time.

(6) This Division applies to a revised corporate plan in the same way it applies to a corporate plan.

34. Matters to be covered by plan

Each corporate plan must include details of the following matters for the period it covers:

(a) a statement of the objectives that Tourism Australia intends to pursue;

(b) the strategies and policies that the Board intends to adopt to achieve Tourism Australia's objectives;

(c) an assessment of the outlook for the Australian tourism industry;

(d) performance indicators for the assessment of Tourism Australia's performance of its functions.

35. Minister's response to corporate plan

(1) The Board must give each corporate plan to the Minister for his or her approval.

(2) The Minister may ask the Board, in writing, to give the corporate plan to the Minister by a time, and in a manner, specified by the Minister. The Board must comply with the request.

(3) The Minister may, by written notice given to the Board:

(a) approve the corporate plan; or

(b) request the Board to revise it for the reasons set out in the request.

(4) The Board must:

(a) comply with the Minister's request to revise the plan; and

(b) give the revised plan to the Minister for his or her approval.

(5) The plan comes into force on the day on which the Board receives written notice of the Minister's approval.

36. Annual operational plan

(1) When the Board is preparing or revising a corporate plan, the Board must:

(a) prepare an annual operational plan for the first financial year to which the corporate plan or revised corporate plan will relate; and

(b) give the plan to the Minister for his or her approval.

(2) The Minister may ask the Board, in writing, to give the annual operational plan to the Minister by a time, and in a manner, specified by the Minister. The Board must comply with the request.

(3) The annual operational plan for a financial year must:

(a) contain an estimate of Tourism Australia's receipts and expenditure for the financial year; and

(b) specify:

(i) the programs that the Board proposes Tourism Australia to carry out; and

(ii) the resources that the Board proposes to allocate to each program; in giving effect to the corporate plan during the financial year.

(4) The Board may revise the annual operational plan on its own initiative at any time.

(5) The Board must give a revised plan to the Minister for his or her approval.

(6) This Division applies to a revised annual operational plan in the same way it applies to an annual operational plan.

37 Minister's response to annual operational plan

(1) The Minister must approve, in writing, an annual operational plan unless the Minister considers that the plan is inconsistent with the corporate plan.

(2) If the Minister considers that the annual operational plan is inconsistent with the corporate plan, the Minister may request the Board, in writing, to revise the annual operational plan.

(3) The Board must:

(a) revise the plan if the Minister requests the Board under subsection (2) to do so and gives reasons in writing to the Board for the request; and

(b) give the revised plan to the Minister for his or her approval.

(4) An annual operational plan comes into force on the day on which the Board receives written notice of the Minister's approval.

38. Board to comply with corporate and annual operational plans

So far as is practicable, the Board must ensure that the performance of Tourism Australia's functions, and the exercise of Tourism Australia's powers, are consistent with, and designed to give effect to, the current corporate plan and the current annual operational plan.

Division 2: Accountability

39. Annual report

The annual report on Tourism Australia under section 9 of the *Commonwealth Authorities and Companies Act 1997* for a period must also include:

(a) an assessment against the performance indicators set out in the corporate plan of the extent to which Tourism Australia's operations during the period have achieved its objectives as stated in the corporate plan; and

(b) an assessment of the extent to which Tourism Australia's operations during the period have implemented each annual operational plan applicable to the period; and

(c) details of:

(i) significant activities undertaken jointly during the period; and

(ii) significant capital works programs undertaken by Tourism Australia during the period; and

(iii) significant acquisitions and dispositions of real property by Tourism Australia during the period; and

(iv) revisions of the corporate plan, and the applicable annual operational plan, approved by the Minister during the period.

40. Ministerial direction

(1) The Minister may give a written direction to the Board in relation to the performance of the functions, and the exercise of the powers, of Tourism Australia.

(2) The Minister must not give a direction to the Board under subsection (1) unless he or she:

(a) has notified the Board in writing that he or she is considering giving the direction; and

(b) has given the Chair an adequate opportunity to discuss with the Minister the need for the proposed direction; and

(c) is satisfied that, because of exceptional circumstances, it is necessary to give the direction to the Board to ensure that the performance of the functions, or the exercise of the powers, of Tourism Australia does not conflict with government policies.

(3) The Board must comply with a direction under subsection (1).

(4) The Minister must cause a copy of a direction under subsection (1):

(a) to be published in the *Gazette* as soon as practicable after giving the direction; and

(b) to be laid before each House of the Parliament within 15 sitting days of that House after giving the direction.

(5) The annual reports of Tourism Australia applicable to periods in which the direction has effect must include:

(a) details of the direction; and

(b) an assessment of the impact that the direction has had on the operations of Tourism Australia during the period.

(6) This section does not affect the application of section 28 of the *Commonwealth Authorities and Companies Act 1997* in relation to Tourism Australia.

Division 3: Tourism Australia Values and Code of Conduct

41. Tourism Australia Values

(1) The Board must determine, in writing, the Tourism Australia Values.

Note: Subsection 33(3) of the *Acts Interpretation Act 1901* provides for the repeal, variation etc. of instruments.

(2) The Board must uphold and promote the Tourism Australia Values.

(3) To avoid doubt, an instrument under subsection (1) is not a legislative instrument for the purposes of the *Legislative Instruments Act 2003*.

42. Tourism Australia Code of Conduct

(1) The Board must determine, in writing, the Tourism Australia Code of Conduct.

Note: Subsection 33(3) of the *Acts Interpretation Act 1901* provides for the repeal, variation etc. of instruments.

(2) The Tourism Australia Code of Conduct applies to the Managing Director and to each employee of Tourism Australia.

(3) To avoid doubt, an instrument under subsection (1) is not a legislative instrument for the purposes of the *Legislative Instruments Act 2003*.

PART 5: MANAGING DIRECTOR, EMPLOYEES AND CONSULTANTS

Division 1: Managing Director

43. Managing Director

There is to be a Managing Director of Tourism Australia.

44. Duties

(1) The Managing Director is to conduct the affairs of Tourism Australia subject to the directions of, and in accordance with policies determined by, the Board.

(2) Anything done by the Managing Director in Tourism Australia's name, or on its behalf is taken to have been done by Tourism Australia.

45. Appointment

(1) The Managing Director is to be appointed by the Board by written instrument.

(2) The Board must not appoint an appointed member as the Managing Director.

(3) The appointment of a person as Managing Director is not invalid because of a defect or irregularity in connection with the person's appointment.

46. Term of appointment

A person appointed as Managing Director holds office for the period specified in the instrument of appointment.

47. Acting Managing Director

(1) The Board may appoint a person (other than a member) to act as the Managing Director:

(a) during a vacancy in the office of Managing

Director (whether or not an appointment has previously been made to the office); or

(b) during any period, or during all periods, when the Managing Director is absent from duty or from Australia, or is, for any reason, unable to perform the duties of the office.

Note: Under section 33A of the *Acts Interpretation Act 1901*, this Act applies in relation to a person acting in a particular office as if the person were the holder of the office.

(2) Anything done by or in relation to a person purporting to act under an appointment is not invalid merely because:

(a) the occasion for the appointment had not arisen; or

(b) there was a defect or irregularity in connection with the appointment; or

(c) the appointment had ceased to have effect; or

(d) the occasion to act had not arisen or had ceased.

48. Remuneration and allowances

(1) The Managing Director is to be paid the remuneration that is determined by the Remuneration Tribunal. If no determination of that remuneration by the Tribunal is in operation, the Managing Director is to be paid the remuneration that is prescribed.

(2) The Managing Director is to be paid the allowances that are prescribed.

(3) This section has effect subject to the *Remuneration Tribunal Act 1973*.

49. Outside employment

The Managing Director must not engage in paid

employment outside the duties of the Managing Director's office without the Board's approval.

50. Recreation leave

The Managing Director has the recreation leave entitlements that are determined by the Remuneration Tribunal.

51. Resignation

The Managing Director may resign his or her appointment by giving the Chair a written resignation.

52. Disclosure of interests

The Managing Director must give written notice to the Chair of all interests (financial or otherwise) that the Managing Director has or acquires and that could conflict with the proper performance of the Managing Director's duties.

53. Termination of appointment

The Board may at any time, in writing, terminate the appointment of the Managing Director.

54. Other terms and conditions

The Managing Director holds office on the terms and conditions (if any) in relation to matters not covered by this Act that are determined by the Board with the Minister's written approval.

Division 2: Employees and consultants

55. Employees

(1) The Board may, on behalf of Tourism Australia, employ such persons as the Board considers necessary for the performance of Tourism Australia's functions and the exercise of Tourism Australia's powers.

(2) An employee is to be employed on the terms and conditions that the Board determines in writing.

56. Consultants

(1) The Board may, on behalf of Tourism Australia, engage persons having suitable qualifications and experience as consultants to the Board.

(2) A consultant is to be engaged on the terms and conditions that the Board determines in writing.

(3) A person does not hold a public office within the meaning of the *Remuneration Tribunal Act 1973* if the person is engaged as a consultant.

PART 6: FINANCE

57. Payments to Tourism Australia by Commonwealth

(1) There is payable to Tourism Australia such money as is appropriated by the Parliament for the purposes of Tourism Australia.

(2) The Finance Minister may give directions about the amounts in which, and the times at which, money payable under subsection (1) is to be paid to Tourism Australia.

(3) In this section:

Finance Minister means the Minister administering the *Financial Management and Accountability Act 1997*.

58. Money of Tourism Australia

(1) The money of Tourism Australia consists of:

(a) money paid to Tourism Australia under section 57; and

(b) any other money paid to Tourism Australia.

(2) The money of Tourism Australia (other than money

vested in Tourism Australia on trust) is to be applied only:

(a) to pay or discharge the costs, expenses and other obligations incurred by Tourism Australia in the performance of its functions and the exercise of its powers; and

(b) to pay any remuneration or allowances payable under this Act.

(3) Subsection (2) does not prevent investment of surplus money of Tourism Australia under section 18 of the *Commonwealth Authorities and Companies Act 1997*.

59. Limits on contracts and leases

(1) Except with the written approval of the Minister, the Board must not:

(a) enter into a contract under which Tourism Australia is to pay or receive an amount exceeding $5,000,000 or, if a higher amount is prescribed, that higher amount; or

(b) enter into a lease of land for a period of 10 years or more.

(2) Paragraph (1)(a) does not apply to the investment of money by Tourism Australia in accordance with section 18 of the *Commonwealth Authorities and Companies Act 1997*.

60. Liability to taxation

(1) Tourism Australia is subject to taxation under the laws of the Commonwealth.

(2) Subject to subsection (3), Tourism Australia is not subject to taxation under a law of a State or Territory.

(3) The regulations may provide that subsection (2)

does not apply in relation to a specified law of a State or Territory.

Note: For specification by class, see subsection 46(2) of the *Acts Interpretation Act 1901.*

61. Trust property

Despite the other provisions of this Act, the Board must deal with any money or property vested in Tourism Australia on trust in accordance with the powers and functions of the Board as trustee.

PART 7: OTHER MATTERS

62. Delegation by Board

(1) The Board may, by resolution of a majority of its members, delegate all or any of its functions or powers to:

(a) a member of the Board; or

(b) a member of staff of Tourism Australia who has the expertise appropriate to the function or power delegated.

(2) In exercising a delegated function or power, the delegate must comply with any written directions of the Board.

(3) The delegation continues in force despite a change in the membership of the Board.

(4) The delegation may be varied or revoked by resolution of the Board (whether or not there has been a change in the membership of the Board).

(5) A certificate signed by the Chair stating any matter with respect to the delegation is prima facie evidence of the matter.

(6) A document purporting to be a certificate mentioned in subsection (5) is taken to be such a certificate

and to have been duly given unless the contrary is established.

63. Delegation by Managing Director

(1) The Managing Director may, in writing, delegate all or any of his or her functions or powers to a member of the Tourism Australia staff who has the expertise appropriate to the function or power delegated.

(2) In performing a delegated function or exercising a delegated power, a delegate must comply with any written directions of the Managing Director.

64. Regulations

The Governor-General may make regulations prescribing matters:

(a) required or permitted by this Act to be prescribed; or

(b) necessary or convenient to be prescribed for carrying out or giving effect to this Act.

THE SCOTTISH NETWORK TOURIST BOARD SCHEME ORDER 2004

Made: 14th September 2004

Laid before the Scottish Parliament: 16th September 2004

Coming into force: 1st December 2004

Schedule 2: Revocations

The Scottish Ministers, in exercise of the powers conferred by sections 172(1), (3) and (4) and 173 of the Local Government etc. (Scotland) Act 1994[1] and of all other powers enabling them in that behalf, after consulting the

Scottish Tourist Board and all local authorities whose areas lie within the area of the Board in accordance with section 173(4)(a) of that Act, hereby make the following Order:

Citation and commencement

1. This Order may be cited as the Scottish Network 1 Tourist Board Scheme Order 2004 and shall come into force on 1st December 2004.

Interpretation

2. In this Order-

"the existing schemes" means-

the Edinburgh and Lothians Tourist Board Scheme 1995;

the Dumfries and Galloway Tourist Board Scheme 1995;

the Greater Glasgow and Clyde Valley Tourist Board Scheme 1995;

the Scottish Borders Tourist Board Scheme 1995; and

the Ayrshire and Arran Tourist Board Scheme 1995;

"the scheme" means the Scottish Network 1 Tourist Board Scheme 2004 set out in Schedule 1 to this Order;

"the Board" means the Scottish Network 1 Tourist Board established under the scheme;

"the existing Boards" means the Edinburgh and Lothians Tourist Board, the Dumfries and Galloway Tourist Board, the Greater Glasgow and Clyde Valley Tourist Board, the Scottish Borders Tourist Board, and the Ayrshire and Arran Tourist Board, established under the existing schemes;

"local government area" shall be construed in accordance with section 1(2) of the Local Government etc. (Scotland) Act 1994; and

"local authority" means a council constituted under section 2 of the Local Government etc. (Scotland) Act 1994.

The scheme

3. - (1) Subject to paragraph (2), the scheme shall have effect, as from 1st April 2005, for the establishment of the Board for the local government areas of City of Edinburgh, East Lothian, Midlothian, West Lothian, Dumfries and Galloway, City of Glasgow, East Dunbartonshire, East Renfrewshire, Inverclyde, North Lanarkshire, Renfrewshire, South Lanarkshire, Scottish Borders, East Ayrshire, North Ayrshire and South Ayrshire.

(2) The scheme shall have effect from the date of coming into force of this Order in relation to-

(a) the constitution of the Board;

(b) the carrying out by the Board of any functions necessary to bring the scheme into operation on 1st April 2005; and

(c) any functions necessary to wind up the existing Boards on 1st April 2005.

Revocations

4. The Orders specified in Schedule 2 to this Order shall be revoked with effect from 1st April 2005.

PART I: GENERAL

1. Title of scheme

This scheme may be cited as the Scottish Network 1 Tourist Board Scheme 2004.

2. Interpretation

(1) In this scheme-

"the 1994 Act" means the Local Government etc. (Scotland) Act 1994; and

"the area of the Board" means the local government areas for which the Board is established under paragraph 3(1).

(2) Any reference in this scheme to a numbered paragraph is a reference to the paragraph in the scheme bearing that number.

PART II: THE CONSTITUTION OF THE BOARD

3. The Board

(1) There shall be established a body to be known as the Scottish Network 1 Tourist Board for the local government areas of City of Edinburgh, City of Glasgow, Dumfries and Galloway, East Ayrshire, East Dunbartonshire, East Lothian, East Renfrewshire, Inverclyde, Midlothian, North Ayrshire, North Lanarkshire, Renfrewshire, Scottish Borders, South Ayrshire, South Lanarkshire and West Lothian.

(2) The Board shall be a body corporate with a common seal.

4. Membership of the Board

(1) The Scottish Ministers shall appoint the first and future members of the Board, which members shall be all or some of the persons who are the members of the Scottish Tourist Board from time to time, as the Scottish Ministers think fit.

(2) The Scottish Ministers may appoint other persons as first or future members of the Board and shall be entitled to remove such persons from membership of the Board, as the Scottish Ministers think fit.

(3) In the case of any member of the Board who is also a member of the Scottish Tourist Board, that member's membership of the Board shall terminate on the termination of that member's membership of the Scottish Tourist Board.

(4) The maximum number of Board members shall be nine.

5. Membership of controlling body

(1) The Scottish Ministers shall appoint the first members of the controlling body of the Board from among the first members of the Board whom they have appointed under paragraph 4.

(2) Subject to sub paragraph (1), the members of the controlling body shall be appointed by the Board from among the members of the Board.

6. Proceedings of the Board

(1) The Board may-

(a) subject to the provisions of this scheme, regulate its own procedure;
(b) appoint committees including committees composed of persons who are not members of the Board;
(c) delegate any of its duties to any of its members who, or committees which are, authorised (generally or specifically) for the purpose;
(d) pay such allowances in respect of expenses as the Board may determine to any of its members or any person appointed to a committee of the Board.

(2) A committee shall act in accordance with such directions as the Board may from time to time give, and the Board may provide for anything done by a committee to have effect as if it had been done by the Board.

(3) The validity of any proceedings of the Board, the controlling body or of any committee appointed by the Board shall not be affected by any vacancy among its members or by any defect in the appointment of any member.

7. Duty to keep accounting records

(1) The Board shall keep accounting records which are sufficient to show and explain the transactions of the Board and are such as to disclose with reasonable accuracy, at any time, the financial position of the Board at that time.

(2) The accounting records of the Board shall at all times be open to inspection by the Scottish Ministers.

(3) Accounting records which the Board is required by sub paragraph (1) to keep shall be preserved by it for three years from the date on which they are made.

PART III: FUNCTIONS AND POWERS OF THE BOARD

8. Additional functions and powers

(1) For the purposes of enabling the Board to carry out its principal function which is specified in section 172(2) of the 1994 Act, but subject to sub paragraph (3), the Board shall have the additional functions and powers conferred upon it by this scheme.

(2) Without prejudice to the generality of sub paragraph (1), the Board shall have power-

(a) to hold property, subject to paragraph 9;

(b) to provide finance, whether by way of grant or loan, to any person in relation to activities relating to tourism;

(c) to borrow such sums as it may require;

(d) to grant security over its assets in respect of obligations incurred by it;

(e) to grant guarantees for obligations (arising out of loans or otherwise) incurred by other persons or grant indemnities;

(f) to enter into contracts with third parties (including the Scottish Tourist Board and any local authority or local authorities) for that third party to carry on activities relating to tourism on behalf of the Board, on such terms and conditions as the Board thinks fit;

(g) to consult, and enter into agreements with, third parties (including the Scottish Tourist Board and any local authority or local authorities) as to the manner in which the Board carries out its activities in relation to tourism; and

(h) to do anything which is calculated to facilitate, or is conducive or incidental to, the discharge of its principal function.

(3) The Board shall not, without the express or general consent given in writing of the Scottish Ministers (or of such body as they may direct the Board to consult) carry on activities relating to the promotion of tourism outside the United Kingdom.

9. Membership, formation and acquisition of companies

(1) The Board may, subject to the conditions specified in this paragraph, form, or join with another person in forming, acquire or become a member of, a company within the meaning of the Companies Act 1985[2].

(2) Subject to sub-paragraph (5), the Board shall itself or together with any other area tourist board established or, as the case may be, approved under sections 172, 173 and 174 of the 1994 Act hold not less than 50 per cent of the voting rights in any company in which it holds an interest.

(3) The memorandum of any company formed or acquired by the Board shall-

(a) enable the company to carry on only activities relating to tourism or such activities as are reasonably incidental to the principal function of the Board; and

(b) provide that the company shall not, without the express or general consent given in writing of Scottish Ministers (or such body as they may direct the Board to consult) carry on activities relating to the promotion of tourism outside the United Kingdom.

(4) In the event that any company formed or acquired by the Board or of which the Board is a member or has an interest of whatsoever nature at any time ceases to comply with the provisions of sub paragraph (3), the Board shall immediately-

(a) take all steps necessary to ensure that the provisions of that sub paragraph are complied with; or

(b) resign from or otherwise terminate its membership of the company, sell or otherwise dispose (other than by way of gift) of any interest which it may have in such company.

(5) Sub-paragraph (2) shall not apply in relation to any interest in a company-

(a) transferred to the Board by virtue of paragraph 13; or

(b) limited by guarantee and established for charitable purposes only.

(6) Sub paragraphs (3) and (4) shall apply in relation to an interest in a company transferred to the Board by virtue

of paragraph 13 only where such interest carries the majority of voting rights in the company.

(7) The Board shall have power to transfer to a company of which it is a member and which complies with the provisions of sub-paragraphs (2) and (3) any or all of such employees of the Board, or such property, rights and liabilities of the Board, as the Board considers appropriate to enable such company to carry out the company's activities in terms of sub-paragraph (3).

10. Staff

(1) The Board may appoint, on such terms and conditions as to remuneration or otherwise as it may determine, such employees as it thinks fit.

(2) The Board may, in the case of such of its employees or former employees as it may determine-

(a) pay such pensions, allowances or gratuities to or in respect of those employees;
(b) make such payments towards provision of such pensions, allowances or gratuities; or
(c) provide and maintain such schemes (whether contributory or not) for the payment of such pensions, allowances or gratuities, as it may determine.

PART IV: TRANSITIONAL PROVISIONS

11. Winding-up and dissolution of existing schemes

Any area tourist board established for the purposes of the exciting schemes revoked under article 4 and Schedule 2 to this Order shall be wound up and dissolved with effect from that date.

12. Transfer of staff

Any person employed on 31st March 2005 by any of the existing Boards wound up and dissolved in accordance with paragraph 11 shall transfer to the employment of the Board on 1st April 2005 on the same terms and conditions as those of his or her employment by the existing Board.

13. Transfer of property, rights and liabilities

On 1st April 2005 there shall transfer to and vest in the Board all property, rights and liabilities of the existing Boards wound up and dissolved in accordance with paragraph 11.

THE WALES TOURIST BOARD (TRANSFER OF FUNCTIONS TO THE NATIONAL ASSEMBLY FOR WALES AND ABOLITION)

Order 2005 (SI 2005/3225)

The functions under the above legislation were delegated to the First Minister by the Assembly in plenary under section 62(1)(b) of the Government of Wales Act 1998 (GoWA) on 22 March 2006. Under section 62(5) of GoWA the First Minister further delegated these functions to the Minister for Economic Development and Transport.

Under Section 63(1)(e) of GoWA the Minister for Economic Development and Transport may delegate these functions to staff. These functions are to be allocated to staff under the Permanent Secretary's arrangements under section 63(2) of GoWA.

Although matters may be delegated for exercise by staff, ultimate responsibility still rests with the Assembly Ministers and through them the First Minister and finally the Assembly. A delegation to staff does not prevent decisions in particular cases being taken by an Assembly Minister, the First Minister or the Assembly itself.

The proposed delegations will become effective from 1 April 2006 and will enable staff to carry out the following functions:

Welsh Development Agency Act 1975

Section 1(3)(a) power to promote Wales as a location for businesses, or assist or concert its promotion as such a location;

Section 1(3)(b) power to provide finance for persons carrying on or intending to carry on businesses;

Section 1(3)(c) power to carry on industrial undertakings and to establish and carry on new businesses; [that only through subsidiaries s.1(5)].

Section 1(3)(d) power to otherwise promote or assist the establishment, growth, modernisation or development of businesses, or a particular business or particular businesses.

Section 1(3)(da) power to make land available for development;

Section 1(3)(f) Power to provide sites, premises, services and facilities for businesses;

Section 1(3)(g) power to manage sites and premises for businesses;

Section 1(3)(h) power to bring derelict land into use or improve its appearance;

Section 1(3)(i) power to undertake the development and re-development of the environment.

Section 1(3)(j) power to promote the private ownership of interests in businesses by the disposal of securities and other property held by the Assembly or any of its subsidiaries.

Section 1(4) a duty to have regard to the requirements of agriculture and efficient land management in the exercise of powers.

Section 1(6) power to do anything to facilitate, incidental or conducive to functions in section 1(3) of the Act.

Section 1(7) Without prejudice to generality of sub-section (6), power in connection with the functions specified in section 1(3) :

- — to acquire, hold and dispose of securities;
- — to form bodies corporate;
- — to form partnerships with other persons;
- — to make loans;
- — to guarantee obligations (arising out of loans or otherwise) incurred by other persons;
- — to make grants;
- — to act as agent for other persons;
- — to acquire and dispose of land, plant, machinery and equipment and other property;
- — to manage land, and to develop land and carry out works on land, and to maintain works or assist in their maintenance;
- — to make land, plant, machinery and equipment and other property available for use by other persons;
- — to provide advisory or other services or facilities in relation to any of their functions, or assist in their provision; and,
- — to promote or assist in the promotion of publicity relating to any of the functions conferred in the Act.

Section 1(14) a duty to consult local government; national park authorities and other bodies with an interest and "from time to time' prepare and publish programmes for the performance of such of its functions under the Act as the Assembly considers appropriate.

Section 4 (a) power to charge for any service provided under the Act;

Section 4 (b) power to accept gifts made for the purpose of exercising functions under the Act, subject appropriate terms and conditions;

Section 4 (c) power to carry out or commission enquiries, investigations or researches deemed necessary or expedient to the exercise of functions under the Act.

Section 5(1) power to appoint a local authority; a national park authority or any other body or person to act as agents of the Assembly in respect of the exercise of functions.

Section 6(1) Power to establish such committees for giving advice to the Assembly about the discharge of any of its functions under the Act as it considers appropriate.

Section 6(2) Power to appoint members of such a committee, who may be either members of the Assembly or persons who are not members.

Section 9(2) power to modernise, adapt and re-construct buildings and power to acquire land as alternative premises for the duration of such works.

Section 9(3) power, in relation to section 9(2), to give special assistance through providing rent free accommodation for an appropriate period of time.

Section 10 power to undertake or assist in the provision of means of access or other services or facilities where expedient for contributing to or supporting the development of business.

Section 13(1) power to make appointments to the Welsh Industrial Development Advisory Board (WIDAB) to advise Assembly in respect of the exercise of its functions under section 7 of the Industrial Development Act 1982.

Section 13(4) a duty to publish a statement in the event of the Assembly deciding under s.7 of the Industrial Development Act 1982 to act contrary to a WIDAB recommendation.

Section 15(1) a duty to prepare and publish programmes for the improvement, development or redevelopment of the environment in Wales;

Section 15(2) power to make payments relating to work contributing to section 15(1) programmes.

Section 16(3) power to:

— pay grants
— acquire land; and
— carry out work

for the purpose of reclaiming/improving and enabling land to come into use that is or is likely to be derelict, neglected or unsightly.

Section 16(7) power to dispose of such land free of charge for use as a public open space.

Section 21A(1) power to acquire land under 1(7)(h) and 16(3)(b) by agreement; compulsorily in respect of Wales; compulsorily in England if authorised by the Secretary of State for Wales.

Section 21A(2) an ancillary power to that in section 21A(1) to acquire either by agreement or compulsorily adjoining land needed to facilitate development or in substitution for common land, allotments.

Section 21A(3) power to acquire rights over land by the creation of new rights (as well as acquiring rights already in existence).

Section 21A(4) a duty to consider certain issues before acquiring such land:

— would land be made available for development without purchase.

— planning permission implications including a requirement to consult every relevant local authority where permission is not available.

— consider the needs of those engaged in building, agriculture, forestry and of the community in general.

Section 21A(6) power to use acquired land for purposes other than the original function intended, so long as the other function is under the Act.

Section 21A(7) a duty to manage acquired land and turn it to account whilst in Assembly possession.

Section 21B a duty not to dispose of land for a consideration less than the best that can be reasonably obtained - except as provided for in Section 16(7) i.e. restored derelict land for use as open space.

Section 21(C) power to advise on and assist in disposal of public authority land; including assistance in making an assessment of the land in their area.

Schedule 3 Para 3 power to borrow money from any person (but borrowing in anything other than sterling to require Treasury Consent) for the purposes of the Act.

Schedule 3 Para 5 a duty on Assembly to ensure that none of its wholly owned subsidiaries borrow money otherwise than from the Assembly, or from another wholly owned subsidiary, except with the Assembly's consent.

Schedule 3 Para 6(4) a duty on the Assembly to make payments in respect of any fulfilment by the Treasury of a guarantee.

Schedule 4 a duty on the Assembly to serve notice

under Schedule 1 to the Acquisition of Land Act 1981 for compulsory purchase order in respect of land acquired under Section 21A.

Schedule 4 Related powers in respect of the acquisition of land by compulsory purchase.

Development of Tourism Act 1969

Section 1(2)(b) power to appoint a member of the British Tourist Authority.

Section 2(1) function to encourage people to visit Wales and the provision and improvement of tourist amenities and facilities.

Section 2(2) power to do anything that is incidental or conducive to the discharge of functions under the Act, and in particular (a) promote and undertake publicity; (b) provide advisory and information services (c) promote or undertake research; establish advisory committees; and contribute to or reimburse expenditure incurred by third parties in respect of (a)-(c).

Section 2(3) power to engage in activities outside the UK for the purpose of encouraging people to visit Wales, on behalf of British Tourist Authority.

Section 2(5) a duty to have regard to co-operating and fostering organisations discharging corresponding functions within Wales together with power to finance or assist such organisations.

Section 2(6) a duty to have regard to the desirability of undertaking appropriate consultation with tourist boards outside Wales and other interested persons and organisations.

Section 2(7A) power to charge for services and receive contributions towards expenses under the Act as read with the Tourism (Overseas Promotion) (Wales) Act 1992.

Section 2 (8A) power to borrow money for the purpose of exercising functions under the Act

Section 3(4) power to impose terms and conditions, including conditions for repayment, in respect of a grant or loan made under any British Tourist Authority scheme under section 3(1) of the Act.

Section 4A(1) power to give financial assistance for projects to improve tourist amenities and facilities in Wales, or to carry out any such project.

Section 4A(2) power to provide financial assistance by means of grant, loan or subscribing or otherwise acquiring shares or stock in a company, or a combination of those methods.

Section 4A(3) power to impose terms and conditions for a project grant, loan or other support arrangements.

Section 4A(4) a duty to consult a relevant company before disposal of relevant shares or stock.

Section 5(1) a duty to advise any Minister of the Crown or public body on such matters relating to tourism in Wales as a whole as may be referred to it or as it may think fit.

Section 17(3)(a) A duty to determine classifications or gradings relating to the registration of hotels and other establishments under an Order in Council.

Section 17(7A) power to publish information relating to a classification register the Assembly holds, either free of charge or for consideration.

Schedule 2 Para 1 (sub paragraphs 1 and 1A) power to require a person in receipt of grant or persons acting on their behalf to furnish information/documentation in order to ensure whether grant conditions have been complied with.

Tourism (Overseas Promotion) (Wales) Act 1992

Section 1(1) power to carry on any activities outside the United Kingdom for the purpose of encouraging people to visit Wales, notwithstanding section 2(3) of the Development of Tourism Act 1969.

International Development Act 2002

Section 9 Subject to the Secretary of State's consent power to carry out agreements for the purpose of furthering sustainable development in one or more countries outside the UK; improving the welfare of the population of one or more such countries; or alleviating the effects of a natural or man-made disaster or other emergency on the population of one or more such country save that the power does not include the provision of financial assistance.

TOURISM NEW SOUTH WALES ACT (1984)

Long Title

An Act to constitute Tourism New South Wales and define its objects and functions; to repeal the *Tourist Industry Development Act 1976*; and for other purposes.

PART 1: PRELIMINARY

1. Name of Act

This Act may be cited as the *Tourism New South Wales Act 1984*.

2. Commencement

(1) Sections 1 and 2 shall commence on the date of assent to this Act.

(2) Except as provided by subsection (1), this Act shall commence on such day as may be appointed by the Governor in respect thereof and as may be notified by proclamation published in the Gazette.

3. Definitions

(1) In this Act, except in so far as the context or subject-matter otherwise indicates or requires:"Chairperson" means the Chairperson of Tourism New South Wales."council" has the same meaning as it has in the *Local Government Act 1993.*"Fund" means the Tourism Development Fund established under section 23."General Manager" means the General Manager of Tourism New South Wales."member" means a member of Tourism New South Wales."part-time member" means a member referred to in section 4 (4) (b)."regulation" means a regulation made under this Act."Tourism New South Wales" means the corporation with the corporate name of "Tourism New South Wales" constituted by this Act.

(2) In this Act, a reference to:

(a) a function includes a reference to a power, authority and duty,

(b) the exercise of a function includes, where the function is a duty, a reference to the performance of the duty, and

(c) facilitating the development of tourism includes a reference to developing tourism.

PART 2: TOURISM NEW SOUTH WALES

4. Constitution of Tourism New South Wales

(1) There is hereby constituted a corporation under the corporate name of "Tourism New South Wales".

(2) Tourism New South Wales:

(a) shall have and may exercise the functions conferred or imposed on it by or under this or any other Act,

(b) shall, for the purposes of any Act, be deemed to be a statutory body representing the Crown, and

(c) shall, in the exercise of its functions (except in

relation to the contents of a report or recommendation made by it to the Minister), be subject to the control and direction of the Minister.

(3) Tourism New South Wales shall consist of not fewer than 7 nor more than 9 members who shall be appointed by the Governor.

(4) Of the members:

(a) one shall, in and by the instrument by which the member is appointed, be appointed as General Manager of Tourism New South Wales, and

(b) the others shall, in and by the instruments by which the members are appointed, be appointed as part-time members.

(5) Schedule 1 has effect with respect to the members.

(6) Schedule 2 has effect with respect to the procedure of Tourism New South Wales.

5. Functions of the General Manager

The General Manager:

(a) is responsible, as the chief executive officer of Tourism New South Wales, for the management of the affairs of Tourism New South Wales subject to and in accordance with the policies and any directions of Tourism New South Wales, and

(b) shall have and may exercise such other functions as are conferred or imposed on the General Manager by or under this or any other Act.

6. (Repealed)

PART 3: FUNCTIONS OF TOURISM NEW SOUTH WALES

7. Objects of Tourism New South Wales

(1) The principal object of Tourism New South Wales is to achieve economic and social benefits for the people of New South Wales through the development of tourism.

(2) Without affecting the generality of subsection (1), Tourism New South Wales shall aim:

(a) to promote travel to and within New South Wales, and

(b) to co-ordinate the development of ventures relating to tourism.

(3) Tourism New South Wales shall determine the policies to be implemented by it in attaining its objects.

8. Powers of Tourism New South Wales

(1) Tourism New South Wales may:

(a) construct, establish, maintain and operate tourist facilities, establish, maintain and conduct enterprises relating to tourism or enter into contracts, agreements or arrangements relating to any one or more of those activities,

(b) provide travel and information services relating to tourism and undertake research into tourism,

(c) market travel and related services,

(d) appoint persons to act as agents of Tourism New South Wales in New South Wales or elsewhere,

(e) act as agent for persons engaged in the provision of travel and tourist facilities and related services,

(f) demand and receive fees, retainers or commissions:

(i) for acting as agent pursuant to the power conferred by paragraph (e),

(ii) for the provision or sale of travel or related services,

(iii) for the provision of tourist facilities or related services, or

(iv) for the provision of any other service by Tourism New South Wales,

(g) borrow money and raise loans under and subject to the *Public Authorities (Financial Arrangements) Act 1987*, and

(h) provide funds for the undertaking of feasibility studies and research relating to the construction, maintenance or improvement of tourist facilities.

(2) Tourism New South Wales may agree to any condition that is not inconsistent with its objects being imposed on its acquisition of any property.

(3) Where, by gift inter vivos, devise or bequest, Tourism New South Wales acquires property, it may retain the property in the form in which it is acquired, except as provided by any condition agreed to by Tourism New South Wales under subsection (2) in relation to the property.

(4) The rule of law against remoteness of vesting does not apply to a condition to which Tourism New South Wales has agreed under subsection (2).

(5) Tourism New South Wales may exercise its functions within or outside New South Wales jointly or in association with any other person (including a corporation constituted otherwise than under an Act of the New South Wales Parliament) situated within New South Wales or elsewhere.

(6) Subject to this Act, Tourism New South Wales shall have such functions, in addition to those specified elsewhere in this Act, as are reasonably necessary for the attainment of its objects.

(7) However, Tourism New South Wales cannot employ any staff.

9. Grants, loans and guarantees—generally

(1) Tourism New South Wales may, with the approval of the Minister:

(a) make a grant or loan, or

(b) execute a guarantee, either alone or jointly with some other person, for the purpose of facilitating the development of tourism.

(2) Subject to section 14, Tourism New South Wales may, in making a grant or loan, or in agreeing to enter into a guarantee, impose such conditions as, in the opinion of Tourism New South Wales, are appropriate.

(3) In this section, "guarantee" means a guarantee of a debt the amount of which is ascertainable when the guarantee is executed.

10. Terms of guarantees

(1) A guarantee executed by Tourism New South Wales is not enforceable against Tourism New South Wales until the creditor has exercised all the rights and remedies of the creditor under all other securities held by or for the creditor in respect of the debt guaranteed.

(2) Tourism New South Wales may, as a condition of a guarantee, require the creditor to obtain, take and hold, or retain and hold, such securities for the payment of the principal debt and interest thereon as Tourism New South Wales requires.

(3) Tourism New South Wales may execute a guarantee notwithstanding that the debt guaranteed includes:

(a) any interest (including compound interest), charges

and expenses chargeable by the creditor against the principal debtor, and

(b) the expenses of enforcing or obtaining or endeavouring to enforce or obtain payment of any amount guaranteed, that interest and those charges and expenses.

(4) Where Tourism New South Wales executes a guarantee, any assignment or encumbrance of the guarantee by the creditor without the consent of Tourism New South Wales has no force or effect.

(5) Tourism New South Wales shall not execute a guarantee:

(a) for the repayment of any money expended or to be expended on:

(i) the acquisition of land, or land and buildings,

(ii) the construction, improvement or alteration of buildings,

(iii) the improvement of land otherwise than as referred to in subparagraph (ii), or

(iv) the acquisition of vehicles, vessels, plant, machinery or equipment, if the amount guaranteed would exceed 90 per cent of:

(v) the estimated value, ascertained as directed by Tourism New South Wales, of the land, or the land and buildings,

(vi) the estimated cost, so ascertained, of the works of construction, improvement or alteration,

(vii) the estimated cost, so ascertained, of the works of improvement, or

(viii) the estimated value, so ascertained, of the vehicles, vessels, plant, machinery or equipment, as the case may be, or

(b) if the amount guaranteed would, together with the amounts of all other guarantees executed by Tourism New South Wales and then in force, or agreed to by Tourism New South Wales but not then executed, exceed such amount as may be determined from time to time by the Treasurer and notified to Tourism New South Wales.

(6) The execution by Tourism New South Wales of a guarantee referred to in this section is, in favour of the creditor, conclusive evidence that the requirements of this section with respect to the guarantee have been complied with.

11. Acquisition of plant and machinery etc

Tourism New South Wales may purchase, lease or exchange, or otherwise acquire, plant, machinery or equipment for the purpose of making it available, on such terms and subject to such conditions as are determined by Tourism New South Wales, to facilitate the development of tourism.

12. Grants and loans

(1) Tourism New South Wales may, with the approval of the Minister, enter into, and give effect to, an agreement with a council to make to the council a grant or loan for the purpose of:

(a) erecting on land vested in the council any building required to facilitate the development of tourism,

(b) altering or extending a building erected on land vested in the council to make it suitable to facilitate the development of tourism,

(c) erecting, on land vested in the council, dwelling houses for occupation by persons employed, or to be employed, on or about a project to facilitate the development of tourism,

(d) improving any land vested in the council to make it suitable for use as a site for a project to facilitate the development of tourism, or

(e) acquiring land for a purpose referred to in paragraph (a), (b), (c) or (d).

(2) Tourism New South Wales may enter into, and give effect to, an agreement with a council for the construction, on land vested in Tourism New South Wales or the council, or in Tourism New South Wales and the council, of buildings suitable to facilitate the development of tourism and the sale, lease or exchange of any such land and buildings.

13. Provision of services

(1) Tourism New South Wales may enter into an agreement with any person with respect to the construction or improvement of roads, works for the supply of water, gas or electricity, or sewerage or drainage works, or other works, whether of the same or of a different kind, to serve any project, being a project to facilitate the development of tourism.

(2) An agreement under this section may provide for:

(a) the whole, or any specified part, of the cost of the roads or other works to be paid by Tourism New South Wales, or

(b) a loan to be made by Tourism New South Wales to meet the whole, or any specified part, of the cost of the roads or other works.

14. Interest on loans and rentals under leases

(1) A loan made by Tourism New South Wales shall be at the rate of interest for the time being fixed by the Treasurer generally for the purposes of this Part or, if the Treasurer so approves, at such rate of interest as may be

fixed by the Treasurer in respect of that loan or without interest.

(2) The rental or other consideration to be received by Tourism New South Wales in respect of a lease of real or personal property acquired for the purposes of this Part shall be fixed by Tourism New South Wales so as to produce an amount per annum which represents not less than such percentage as the Minister may direct, in respect of that lease, or of leases of the class to which that lease belongs, of the value of the real or personal property leased.

15. (Repealed)

PART 4: ACQUISITION OF LAND

16. Acquisition of land

Tourism New South Wales may:

(a) for the purpose of providing a site for a project, being a project to facilitate the development of tourism, or a site that, in the opinion of Tourism New South Wales, is likely to be required for such a project, and

(b) with the approval of the Minister, acquire land (including an interest in land) by agreement or by compulsory process in accordance with the *Land Acquisition (Just Terms Compensation) Act 1991.*

17. Application of the Public Works Act 1912

(1) For the purposes of the *Public Works Act 1912*, any acquisition of land under section 16 is taken to be for an authorised work and the Corporation is, in relation to that authorised work, taken to be the Constructing Authority.

(2) Sections 34, 35, 36 and 37 of the *Public Works Act 1912* do not apply in relation to works constructed under this Act.

18. Subdivision

Tourism New South Wales may cause a plan to be made of any land acquired by Tourism New South Wales under this Part showing the proposed roads and reserves for public recreation or other public purposes, and the land to be set apart as sites for buildings or works.

19. Improvements and dedication

(1) Tourism New South Wales may:

(a) cause any work to be done on or in relation to any land acquired by Tourism New South Wales pursuant to this Part for the purpose of improving it to make it suitable to be used as a site for a project to facilitate the development of tourism or for a dwelling house for occupation by a person employed or to be employed on or about any such project,

(b) dedicate by notification in the Gazette any such land as a reserve for public recreation or for other public purposes, and fence, plant and improve any such reserve, and by notification in the Gazette vest the reserve in the council of the area in which it is situated or in trustees, and

(c) set apart any such land as sites for buildings or works or for local government purposes.

(2) Where any reserve is vested under this section, the provisions of the *Crown Lands Consolidation Act 1913* apply to and in respect of the reserve in the same way as they apply to and in respect of land dedicated and vested under that Act.

20. Tourism New South Wales as Constructing Authority

For the purposes of section 81 of the *Public Works Act 1912*, Tourism New South Wales shall be deemed to be a Constructing Authority.

21 Erection, alteration and extension of buildings

(1) Tourism New South Wales may cause to be erected, on land acquired by Tourism New South Wales under this Part for the purpose referred to in section 16, buildings suitable to facilitate the development of tourism.

(2) Tourism New South Wales may cause any building erected on land acquired by Tourism New South Wales under this Part for the purpose referred to in section 16 to be altered or extended to make it suitable to facilitate the development of tourism.

22. Disposal of land

(1) Tourism New South Wales, with the approval of the Minister, may, in such manner and subject to such terms and conditions as in the opinion of Tourism New South Wales are appropriate, sell, lease, exchange or otherwise deal with or dispose of any real or personal property that has been acquired by Tourism New South Wales under this Part and grant easements or rights-of-way over any land or any part thereof that has been so acquired by Tourism New South Wales.

(2) Any money received by Tourism New South Wales in respect of any transaction that is entered into by Tourism New South Wales under subsection (1) and that relates to any land acquired by Tourism New South Wales for the purpose referred to in section 16 shall be paid into the Fund.

PART 5: FINANCE

23. Tourism Development Fund

(1) There shall be established and maintained in the Special Deposits Account in the Treasury a Tourism Development Fund into which shall be paid:

(a) from the Country Industries Assistance Fund in the Special Deposits Account in the Treasury such amounts as are from time to time agreed upon by the Minister and the Minister administering the *State Development and Industries Assistance Act 1966*, the payment of which from that Fund is hereby authorised,

(b) any money appropriated by Parliament for the purposes of the Fund,

(c) money borrowed by Tourism New South Wales,

(d) principal money repaid in respect of loans referred to in subsection 2 (d) and interest received in respect of any such loan,

(e) the proceeds of any transaction affecting real or personal property acquired with money from the Fund, and

(f) such fees or other amounts received by Tourism New South Wales as may be determined by the Minister with the concurrence of the Treasurer.

(2) Money in the Fund may be expended by Tourism New South Wales for the purpose of:

(a) discharging such commitments of the Country Industries Assistance Fund with respect to tourism as were outstanding immediately before the payment into the Fund of the amounts referred to in subsection (1) (a),

(b) paying such of the expenses of administering this Act as relate to the collection and expenditure of money in the Fund,

(c) promoting and assisting the development of tourism,

(d) making grants or loans in aid of projects to facilitate the development of tourism and becoming a member of a company where, in the opinion of the Minister, the company's objects provide principally for projects of that kind,

(e) repaying money borrowed by Tourism New South Wales, paying interest on money so borrowed and paying the expenses of Tourism New South Wales in borrowing money,

(f) discharging any liability of Tourism New South Wales under a guarantee given by Tourism New South Wales,

(g) paying any money for which Tourism New South Wales is liable under the *Capital Debt Charges Act 1957*,

(h) acquiring land pursuant to Part 4, and

(i) making any other payments that Tourism New South Wales is, by or under this Act or the regulations, required or authorised to make from the Fund.

(3) Tourism New South Wales shall, at such times as the Treasurer directs, pay to the Treasurer such part as the Treasurer specifies, when given the direction, of money paid as interest on any transaction referred to in subsection (1) (e) or on loans made under subsection (2) (d), other than loans made from money borrowed by Tourism New South Wales.

(4) There shall be paid, at such times as the Treasurer directs, from the Fund to the Treasurer for credit of the Consolidated Fund such percentage of such income, or such classes or descriptions of income, received by Tourism New South Wales as may be prescribed.

(5) In subsection (4), "income" includes, but is not limited to:

(a) rentals or other consideration in respect of leases, and

(b) fees or other revenue in respect of licences or agreements.

24. Financial year

The financial year of Tourism New South Wales shall be the year commencing on 1 July.

PART 6: MISCELLANEOUS

25. Disclosure of information

A person shall not disclose any information obtained in connection with the administration or execution of this Act (or any other Act conferring or imposing functions on Tourism New South Wales) unless that disclosure is made:

(a) with the consent of the person from whom the information was obtained,
(b) in connection with the administration or execution of this Act (or any such other Act),
(c) for the purposes of any legal proceedings arising out of this Act (or any such other Act) or of any report of any such proceedings,
(d) in accordance with a requirement made under the *Ombudsman Act 1974*, or
(e) with other lawful excuse.

26. Delegation

(1) Tourism New South Wales may, by instrument in writing, delegate to:

(a) the General Manager,
(b) a committee comprised of members, including the General Manager or a member nominated by the General Manager,
(c) an officer or temporary employee of Tourism New South Wales,

(d) a person for the time being holding or acting in a specified position in the staff establishment of Tourism New South Wales, or

(e) any person of whose services Tourism New South Wales makes use pursuant to this or any other Act, the exercise of such of the functions of Tourism New South Wales (other than this power of delegation) as are specified in the instrument.

(2) A function the exercise of which has been delegated under this section may, while the delegation remains unrevoked, be exercised from time to time by the delegate in accordance with the terms of the delegation.

(3) Without limiting the operation of subsection (2), a function the exercise of which has been delegated under this section to the General Manager may, while the delegation remains unrevoked, be exercised from time to time in accordance with the terms of the delegation by:

(a) an officer or temporary employee of Tourism New South Wales,

(b) a person for the time being holding or acting in a specified position in the staff establishment of Tourism New South Wales, or

(c) any person of whose services Tourism New South Wales makes use pursuant to this or any other Act, as authorised by instrument in writing by the General Manager in that behalf either generally or in a particular case or class of cases.

(4) A delegation or authorisation under this section may be made subject to such conditions or limitations as to the exercise of any function the subject thereof, or as to time or circumstances, as may be specified in the instrument of delegation or authorisation.

(5) Notwithstanding any delegation under this section, Tourism New South Wales may continue to exercise any function delegated.

(6) Any act or thing done or suffered by a delegate acting in the exercise of a delegation under this section, or by a person duly authorised in that behalf by the General Manager under this section, has the same force and effect as it would have if it had been done or suffered by Tourism New South Wales and shall be deemed to have been done or suffered by Tourism New South Wales.

(7) Tourism New South Wales may, by instrument in writing, revoke wholly or in part any delegation under this section, and the General Manager may, by instrument in writing, revoke wholly or in part any authorisation under this section.

(8) An instrument purporting to have been signed by a person in the capacity of delegate of Tourism New South Wales, or as a person authorised under this section, shall in all courts and before all persons acting judicially be received in evidence as if it were an instrument duly executed by Tourism New South Wales and shall, until the contrary is proved, be deemed to be an instrument signed by a delegate of Tourism New South Wales or by a person duly authorised under this section, as the case may be.

(9) In subsection (8), a reference to a delegate includes a reference to the chairperson of a committee to which the exercise of a function has been delegated under subsection (1).

27. Annual report

(1) As soon as practicable after 30 June, but on or before 31 December, in each year, Tourism New South Wales shall prepare and forward to the Minister a report of its work and activities for the 12 months ending on 30 June in that year.

(2) The Minister shall lay the report or cause it to be laid before both Houses of Parliament as soon as practicable after receiving the report.

28. References to Tourism New South Wales

In any other Act, in any instrument made under any Act or in any other instrument of any kind, except in so far as the context or subject-matter otherwise indicates or requires, a reference to the "Tourism Commission", to the "Tourism Commission of New South Wales" or to the "NSW Tourism Commission" shall be read and construed as a reference to Tourism New South Wales constituted by this Act.

29. Service of documents

(1) A document may be served on Tourism New South Wales by leaving it at, or by sending it by post to:

(a) the office of Tourism New South Wales, or

(b) if it has more than one office—any one of its offices.

(2) Nothing in subsection (1) affects the operation of any provision of a law or of the rules of a court authorising a document to be served on Tourism New South Wales in a manner not provided for by subsection (1).

30. Authentication of certain documents

Every summons, process, demand, order, notice, statement, direction or document requiring authentication by Tourism New South Wales may be sufficiently authenticated without the seal of Tourism New South Wales if signed by the General Manager or by any officer or temporary employee of Tourism New South Wales authorised to do so by the General Manager.

31. Recovery of charges etc by Tourism New South Wales

Any charge, fee or money due to Tourism New South

Wales may be recovered by Tourism New South Wales as a debt in a court of competent jurisdiction.

32. Proof of certain matters not required

In any legal proceedings, no proof shall be required (until evidence is given to the contrary) of:

(a) the constitution of Tourism New South Wales,
(b) any resolution of Tourism New South Wales,
(c) the appointment of, or the holding of office by, any member, or
(d) the presence or nature of a quorum at any meeting of Tourism New South Wales.

33. Proceedings for offences

Proceedings for an offence against this Act may be taken before a Local Court constituted by a Magistrate sitting alone.

34. Regulations

(1) The Governor may make regulations, not inconsistent with this Act, for or with respect to any matter that by this Act is required or permitted to be prescribed or that is necessary or convenient to be prescribed for carrying out or giving effect to this Act.

(2) A provision of a regulation may:

(a) apply generally or be limited in its application by reference to specified exceptions or factors,
(b) apply differently according to different factors of a specified kind, or
(c) authorise any matter or thing to be from time to time determined, applied or regulated by any specified person or body, or may do any combination of those things.

35. Repeals

Each Act specified in Schedule 3 is, to the extent specified in that Schedule in relation to that Act, repealed.

36. Savings and transitional provisions

Schedule 4 has effect.

SCHEDULE 1 PROVISIONS RELATING TO THE MEMBERS OF TOURISM NEW SOUTH WALES

(Section 4 (5))

1A. Employment of General Manager

The employment of the General Manager is subject to Part 2A of the *Public Sector Management Act 1988*, but is not subject to Part 2 of that Act.

1. (Repealed)

2. Chairperson of Tourism New South Wales

(1) Of the part-time members, one shall, in and by the relevant instrument of appointment as such a member, or by another instrument executed by the Governor, be appointed as Chairperson of Tourism New South Wales.

(2) The Governor may remove a part-time member from the office of Chairperson.

(3) A person who is a part-time member and Chairperson shall be deemed to have vacated office as Chairperson if the person:

(a) is removed from that office by the Governor under subclause (2),

(b) resigns that office by instrument in writing addressed to the Minister, or

(c) ceases to be a part-time member.

3. Acting members and acting Chairperson

(1) The Governor may, from time to time, appoint a person to act in the office of a member during the illness or absence of the member, and the person, while so acting, shall have and may exercise all the functions of the member.

(2) The Governor may, from time to time, appoint a part-time member to act in the office of Chairperson during the illness or absence of the Chairperson, and the part-time member, while so acting, shall have and may exercise all the functions of the Chairperson.

(3) The Governor may remove any person from any office to which the person was appointed under subclause (1) or (2).

(4) A person while acting in the office of a member is entitled to be paid such remuneration (including travelling and subsistence allowances) as the Minister may from time to time determine in respect of the person.

(5) For the purposes of this clause:

(a) a vacancy in the office of a member or the Chairperson shall be deemed to be an absence from office of the member or Chairperson, as the case may be, and

(b) a part-time member shall be deemed to be absent from office as a part-time member during any period that the member acts in the office of the General Manager pursuant to an appointment under subclause (1).

(6) In subclause (2), clauses 9 and 10 and Schedule 2:

(a) a reference to a member or part-time member includes a reference to a person acting in the office of a member or part-time member,

(b) a reference to the appointment of a member includes a reference to the appointment of a person to act in the office of a member, and

(c) a reference to the office of a member or part-time member includes a reference to the office of a person appointed to act in the office of a member or part-time member.

4. Term of office

Subject to this Schedule, a part-time member holds office for such term (not exceeding 5 years) as may be specified in the member's instrument of appointment, but is eligible (if otherwise qualified) for re-appointment.

5. (Repealed)

6. Remuneration

(1) (Repealed)

(2) A part-time member is entitled to be paid such remuneration (including travelling and subsistence allowances) as the Minister may from time to time determine in respect of the part-time member.

7. Filling of vacancy in office of member

In the event of the office of any member becoming vacant a person shall, subject to this Act, be appointed to fill the vacancy.

8. Casual vacancies

(1) A part-time member shall be deemed to have vacated office if the member:

(a) dies,

(b) (Repealed)

(c) absents himself or herself from 4 consecutive meetings of Tourism New South Wales of which reasonable notice has been given to the member personally or in the ordinary course of post, except on leave granted by the Minister (which leave the Minister is hereby authorised to grant) or unless, before the expiration of 4 weeks after the last of those meetings, the member is excused by the Minister for being absent from those meetings,

(d) becomes bankrupt, applies to take the benefit of any law for the relief of bankrupt or insolvent debtors, compounds with his or her creditors or makes an assignment of his or her remuneration for their benefit,

(e) becomes a temporary patient, a continued treatment patient, a protected person or an incapable person within the meaning of the *Mental Health Act 1958* or a person under detention under Part 7 of that Act,

(f) is convicted in New South Wales of an offence which is punishable by imprisonment for 12 months or upwards, or is convicted elsewhere than in New South Wales of an offence which if committed in New South Wales would be an offence so punishable,

(g) (Repealed)

(h) resigns the office by instrument in writing addressed to the Minister, or

(i), (j) (Repealed)

(k) is removed by the Governor under this clause or under Part 8 of the *Public Sector Management Act 1988*.

(2), (3) (Repealed)

(4) The Governor may remove a part-time member from office.

(5) (Repealed)

9. Disclosure of pecuniary interests

(1) A member who has a direct or indirect pecuniary interest:

(a) in a matter that is being considered, or is about to be considered, at a meeting of Tourism New South Wales, or

(b) in a thing being done or about to be done by Tourism New South Wales, shall, as soon as possible after the relevant facts have come to the member's knowledge, disclose the nature of the interest at a meeting of Tourism New South Wales.

(2) A disclosure by a member at a meeting of Tourism New South Wales that the member:

(a) is a member, or is in the employment, of a specified company or other body,

(b) is a partner, or is in the employment, of a specified person, or

(c) has some other specified interest relating to a specified company or other body or a specified person, shall be deemed to be a sufficient disclosure of the nature of the interest in any matter or thing relating to that company or other body or to that person which may arise after the date of the disclosure.

(3) Tourism New South Wales shall cause particulars of any disclosure made under subclause (1) or (2) to be recorded in a book kept for the purpose and that book shall be open at all reasonable hours to the inspection of any person on payment of such fee as may be determined by Tourism New South Wales from time to time.

(4) After a member has, or is deemed to have, disclosed the nature of an interest in any matter or thing pursuant

to subclause (1) or (2), the member shall not, unless the Minister otherwise determines:

(a) be present during any deliberation of Tourism New South Wales, or take part in any decision of Tourism New South Wales, with respect to that matter, or

(b) exercise any function under this Act with respect to that thing, as the case may require.

(5) Notwithstanding that a member contravenes the provisions of this clause, that contravention does not invalidate any decision of Tourism New South Wales or the exercise of any function under this Act.

(6) Nothing in this clause applies to or in respect of an interest of a member in a matter or thing which arises by reason only that the member is a member of any body concerned in the promotion of tourism.

(7) A reference in this clause to a meeting of Tourism New South Wales includes a reference to a meeting of a committee of Tourism New South Wales.

10. Effect of certain other Acts

(1) The *Public Service Act 1979* does not apply to or in respect of the appointment of a part-time member and a part-time member is not, as a member, subject to that Act.

(2) Where by or under any other Act provision is made requiring a person who is the holder of an office specified therein to devote the whole of his or her time to the duties of that office, or prohibiting the person from engaging in employment outside the duties of that office, that provision shall not operate to disqualify the person from holding that office and also the office of a part-time member or from accepting and retaining any remuneration payable to the person under this Act as a part-time member.

(3) The office of a part-time member shall for the purposes of any Act be deemed not to be an office or place of profit under the Crown.

11-13. (Repealed)

14. Liability of members etc

No matter or thing done by Tourism New South Wales, and no matter or thing done by any member or by any person acting under the direction of Tourism New South Wales shall, if the matter or thing was done bona fide for the purposes of executing this or any other Act, subject a member or a person so acting personally to any action, liability, claim or demand whatever.

SCHEDULE 2 PROVISIONS RELATING TO THE PROCEDURE OF TOURISM NEW SOUTH WALES

(Section 4 (6))

1. General procedure

The procedure for the calling of meetings of Tourism New South Wales and for the conduct of business at those meetings shall, subject to this Act, be as determined by Tourism New South Wales.

2 Quorum

A majority of the members shall form a quorum and any duly convened meeting of Tourism New South Wales at which a quorum is present shall be competent to transact any business of Tourism New South Wales and shall have and may exercise all the functions of Tourism New South Wales.

3 Presiding member

(1) The Chairperson or, in the absence of the Chairperson, another part-time member elected as chairperson for the

meeting by the members present shall preside at a meeting of Tourism New South Wales.

(2) The person acting as chairperson at any meeting of Tourism New South Wales shall have a deliberative vote and, in the event of an equality of votes, shall have a second or casting vote.

4 Voting

A decision supported by a majority of the votes cast at a meeting of Tourism New South Wales at which a quorum is present shall be the decision of Tourism New South Wales.

5 Minutes

Tourism New South Wales shall cause full and accurate minutes to be kept of the proceedings of each meeting of Tourism New South Wales.

SCHEDULE 3: *REPEALS*

(Section 35)

Tourist Industry Development Act 1976 No 58 —the whole Act.

Miscellaneous Acts (Financial Accommodation) Amendment Act 1981 No 83 —so much of Schedule 1 as amends the *Tourist Industry Development Act 1976*.

Tourist Industry Development (Amendment) Act 1982 No 172 —the whole Act.

Tourist Industry Development (Amendment) Act 1983 No 74 —the whole Act.

Tourist Industry Development (Further Amendment) Act 1983 No 141 —the whole Act.

SCHEDULE 4: SAVINGS AND TRANSITIONAL PROVISIONS

1. Definitions

In this Schedule:

"appointed day" means the day appointed and notified under section 2 (2).

"former Act" means the *Tourist Industry Development Act 1976*.

"new corporation" means Tourism New South Wales.

"old corporation" means the corporation constituted by section 5 of the *Tourist Industry Development Act 1976*.

2. Continuity of corporation

The new corporation is a continuation of, and the same legal entity as, the old corporation.

3. References to old corporation

On and from the appointed day, a reference in any Act, in any instrument made under any Act or in any other instrument of any kind (enacted, made or executed before the appointed day) to the old corporation shall be read and construed as a reference to the new corporation.

4. Activities commenced by old corporation

(1) Any act, matter or thing done or commenced to be done under a provision of the former Act or any other Act by or in relation to the old corporation before the appointed day shall be deemed to have been done or commenced to be done and, in the latter case, may be completed, under the corresponding provision of this Act or the provision of the other Act, as the case may be, by or in relation to the new corporation.

(2) Nothing in subclause (1) affects the operation of Schedule 2 to the *Miscellaneous Acts (Financial Accommodation) Amendment Act 1981* with respect to the old corporation.

5. First meeting of new corporation

The Minister shall call the first meeting of the new corporation on or after the appointed day in such manner as the Minister thinks fit.

6. Disposition of former Fund

The Tourist Industry Development Fund established under the former Act shall be deemed to have been established under section 23 as the Tourism Development Fund.

7. Saving of certain amendments

The repeal of the former Act by this Act does not affect the amendments made:

(a) to the *Local Government Act 1919*, by section 30 of the former Act, or

(b) to the *Government Guarantees Act 1934*, by section 31 of the former Act.

8 Regulations

(1) The Governor may make regulations containing provisions of a savings or transitional nature consequent on the enactment of this Act.

(2) A provision made under subclause (1) may take effect as from the appointed day or a later day.

(3) To the extent to which a provision referred to in subclause (1) takes effect from a date that is earlier than the date of its publication in the Gazette, the provision does not operate so as:

(a) to affect, in a manner prejudicial to any person (other than the State or an authority of the State), the rights of that person existing before the date of its publication therein, or

(b) to impose liabilities on any person (other than the State or an authority of the State) in respect of anything done or omitted to be done before the date of its publication therein.

(4) A provision made under subclause (1) shall, if the regulations under this clause so provide, have effect notwithstanding any other clause of this Schedule (clause 2 excepted).

8

Select Visa Rules, Global Holidays Act & Tourism Law

SRI LANKA VISA RULES

There are different types of Sri Lanka visas but the most common visa for touring Sri Lanka is a single entry tourist visa, which is valid for up to one month. A Sri Lanka visa for overseas passport holders is required when traveling to the country. Visa regulations are simple. Tourists visiting Srilanka can enter the country with minimum formalities.

Citizens of following 77 countries can enter Sri Lanka without a prior visa and will be allowed an entry visa for between 30-90 days (depending on country of nationality) at the point of entry without any payment.

1. Albania, 2. Armenia, 3. Australia, 4. Austria, 5. Azerbaijan, 6. Bahrain, 7. Bangladesh, 8. Belarus, 9. Belgium, 10. Bhutan, 11. Bosnia-Herzegovina, 12. Brunei, 13. Bulgaria, 14. Canada, 15. China, 16. Croatia, 17. Cyprus, 18. Czech, Republic, 19. Denmark, 21. Estonia, 22. Finland, 23. France, 24. Georgia, 25. Germany, 26. Greece, 27. Hong Kong, 28. Hungary, 29. India, 30. Indonesia, 31. Iran, 32. Ireland, 33. Israel, 34. Italy, 35. Japan, 36. Kazakhstan, 37. Kyrgyz Stan, 38. Kuwait, 39. Latvia, 40. Luxembourg, 41. Macedonia, 42. Maldives, 43. Malaysia, 44. Moldova, 45. Netherlands, 46.

New Zealand, 47. Nepal, 48. Norway, 49. Oman, 50. Pakistan, 51. Philippines, 52. Poland, 53. Portugal, 54. Romania, 55. Russian Federation, 56. Saudi Arabia, 57. Serbia-Montenegro, 58. Seychelles, 59. Slovakia, 60. Slovenia, 61. South Africa, 62. South Korea, 63. Spain, 64. Sweden, 65. Switzerland, 66. Taiwan, 67. Tajikistan, 68. Thailand, 69. Turkey, 70. Turkmenistan, 71. U.A.E., 72. U.K., 73. Ukraine, 74. U.S.A., 75. Uzbekistan

Nationals of countries not classified under the above 77 countries are required to possess a valid visa, obtained from the respective Sri Lanka Diplomatic Missions, prior to entering the country irrespective of the purpose of visit. Tourists should have a return air ticket, sufficient foreign exchange @ US$ 30/- per day, and valid travel documents to establish their bona-fide as tourists.

The Sri Lanka business visa is usually issued for a single entry within 90 days provided the passport remains valid, for a period of stay not exceeding 30 days. Three months multiple entries visa is available on request. Passport must have at least six months validity beyond entry date and must contain at least one blank visa page for visa to be issued.

For obtaining business visa, a business letter of responsibility typewritten on official letterhead is required and it should be addressed to the Sri Lankan embassy in the concerned country.

The letter must state all of the following:

- The nature of the business to be performed
- The name of the business reference to be visited
- Guarantee sufficient financial support for the visit
- Guarantee return transportation to the country of origin

Your sponsor letter should be signed by a company officer other than the applicant.

Your sponsor in Sri Lanka must send a fax to the Embassy

of Sri Lanka in the country of origin, stating the name of the applicant, confirming the business trip (fax must include company address and type of business). For stay over 7 days, the letter must be sent via the Immigration Department in Colombo.

MYANMAR TOURISM LAW

The State Law and Order Restoration Council Myanmar Tourism Law

The State Law and Order Restoration Council Law No. 13/90.

The 13th Waning Day of Nayon, 1352 ME. (20th June, 1990).

The State Law and Order Restoration Council hereby enacts the following Law :-

CHAPTER I: TITLE AND DEFINITION

1. This Law shall be called the Myanmar Tourism Law.

2. The following expressions contained in this Law shall have the meanings given hereunder

a. Tourist means a person travelling from his place of residence to another place for a visit. This expression also includes a domestic tourist, international tourist and a foreign visitor;

b. Tourism Industry includes tourist enterprise, hotel business, lodging-house business, tourist transport business, tour guide business and business which are prescribed by the Myanmar Tourism Commission as tourism industry;

c. Tourist Enterprise means an economic enterprise which a tour operator business or travel agency business or both;

d. Hotel Business means an economic enterprise, which provides accommodation and food, beverage and other services for tourists. This expression also includes restaurant business opened at the hotel or within its premises;

e. Lodging House Business means an economic enterprise, which provides only accommodation for tourists. This expression also includes guesthouse business, boarding-house business or similar lodging business;

f. Tourist Transport Business means an economic enterprise, which provides transport to tourists within a town or from one town to another or to any locality within the country;

g. Tour Guide Business means an economic enterprise, which provides tour service to tourists;

h. Commission means the Myanmar Tourism Commission formed under this Law;

i. Directorate means the Directorate formed by the Government under this Law;

j. Inspector means the Directorate or a person assigned by the Directorate in order to inspect tourism industry contained in this Law;

k. License means a permit issued by the Directorate to operate any t~in5m industry;

l. License-ho1der means a person who has the right to operate any tourism industry under this Law

CHAPTER II: BASIC PRINCIPLES

3. Tourism industry shall be operated in accordance with the following basic principles: -

a. prevention of infringement of the sovereignty and security of the State;

b. betterment of the interests of Myanmar and its citizens;
c. contributing to the friendship, understanding and unity of the national races through tourism industry;
d. preservation and development of ancient historical sites and monuments, traditional arts and custom of the national races, which are the cultural heritage of Myanmar;
e. preservation and development of natural scenic beauty and natural environmental heritage of Myanmar;
f. contributing to international friendship and understanding through tourism industry;
g. development of technical knowledge relating to tourism industry and opening up of more employment opportunities;
h. providing security and satisfaction of tourists.

CHAPTER III: FORMATION, DUTIES AND POWERS OF THE COMMISSION

4. The Government shall, by notification form the Myanmar Tourism Commission

5. The duties and powers of the Commission are as follows:

-

a. laying down the policies of Tourism;
b. causing the implementation of the systematic development of the to tourism industry;
c. designating of areas in which cultural and natural heritage exist as tourism zones;
d. giving guidelines for international relations with regard to the tourism industry;
e. giving guidelines for improving the quality and raising the standard of tourism industry and

dissemination of technical knowledge relating thereto;

f. determining an economic enterprise operating any of the services such as health, knowledge, recreation, and entertainment for tourists as a tourism industry;

g. submitting to the government from time to time the activities carried out;

h. carrying out the duties and powers assigned from time to time by the Government.

CHAPTER IV: APPLICATION FOR LICENSE

6. A person desirous of operating any of the following businesses of tourism industry for international tourists or foreign visitors shall apply for a license to the Directorate in the prescribed form-

a. Tourist Enterprise;

b. Hotel Business;

c. Lodging-House Business;

a. Tourist transport Business;

e. Tour Guide Business;

f. Businesses prescribed from time to time as a Tourism Industry by the Commission.

7. The Directorate may prescribe the types of business to be operated under a license for domestic tourists from among the businesses contained in section 6.

CHAPTER V: DUTIES AND RIGHTS OF THE LICENSE-HOLDER

8. The license-holder shall pay the license fee and other duties and taxes prescribed by the Directorate.

9. The license-holder shall abide by the conditions contained in the license.

10. The license-holder shall abide by the order, notification and directives issued from time to time by the Commission or the Directorate,

11. The license-holder dissatisfied with the order or decision of the Directorate relating to the license has the right to file an appeal to the Minister of the Ministry concerned.

CHAPTER VI: FORMATION, DUTIES AND POWERS OF THE DIRECTORATE

12. In order to operate the Tourism Industry systematically in accordance with the provision of this Law, the government shall form a Directorate

13. The duties and powers of the Directorate are as follows:

a. carrying out in accordance with the policies laid down by the Commission;
b. implementing for the systematic development of the tourism industry;
c. carrying out for the promotion of the tourism industry;
d. carrying out to improve the quality and to raise the standard of tourism industry and to disseminate technical knowledge relating thereto;
e. supervising the tourism industry in accordance with the provisions of this Law;
f. prescribing and revising the license fee and
g. other taxes and duties;
h. issuing, refusing, suspending, revoking or canceling the license;
i. appointing Inspectors to inspect the tourism industry;
j. carrying out the duties and powers assigned from

time to time by the Commission and the Ministry concerned.

14. The Directorate may, in consultation with the departments concerned stipulate conditions relating to foreign currency earned by the license-holder from the tourism industry.

CHAPTER VII: INSPECTION AND TAKING OF ACTION

15. The Inspector shall carry out the following duties: -

a. inspecting the tourism industry within the area for which he has undertaken responsibility or within the area specially assigned and investigating as may be necessary;
b. taking action in accordance with the procedures against a person who has violated any prohibition contained in this Law;
c. carrying out duties assigned from time to time by the Directorate.

16. The powers of the Inspector are as follows: -

a. calling for and copying records, accounts and other supporting documents relating to the industry, and inspecting articles relating to the industry in order to examine whether or not a license-holder has complied with the conditions of the license;
b. having the right to examine in accordance with this Law any building, vehicle or person relating to the tourism industry.

CHAPTER VIII: INVALIDATION OF LICENSE

17. The License is invalidated when any of the following events occur:

a. death of the license-bolder;
b. expiry of the term of the license;
c. revocation or cancellation of the license;
d. surrender of the license by the license-holder when he wishes to discontinue his business.

18. If the Directorate finds after investigation that the license-holder has discontinued his business, the said license may be deemed to have become invalidated.

19. The license-holder shall surrender the license invalidated under section 17 to the Directorate or the State/Division, Township Zone or Township Office of the Directorate within 15 days from the date on which it was invalidated.

CHAPTER IX: APPEALS

20. An applicant for a license or a license-holder dissatisfied with the order or decision passed by the Directorate may file an appeal to the Minister concerned within 30 days of the receipt of such order or decision.

21. The decision of the Minister concerned shall be final.

CHAPTER X: PROHIBITIONS

22. No one shall engage in any tourism industry under section 6 or section 7 without a license.

23. A license-holder-

a. shall not violate any condition contained in the license;
b. shall not violate any prohibition contained in an order, notification or directive issued from time to time by the Commission or the Directorate.

24. No one shall interfere or obstruct the Inspector in the discharge of his duties.

25. No one shall form an association relating to the tourism industry without registering in accordance with the Myanmar Companies Act.

CHAPTER XI: OFFENCES AND PENALTIES

26. Whoever violates the provision of section 22 shall, on conviction be punished with imprisonment for a term which may extend to 3 years or with fine which may extend to kyats 30,000 or with both.

27. A license-holder who violates the provision of section 23 shall, on conviction be punished with imprisonment for a term which may extend to 2 years or with fine which may extend to kyats 20,000 or with both.

28. Whoever violates the provision of section 24 shall, on conviction be punished with imprisonment for a term which may extend to 2 years or with fine which may extend to kyats 20,000 or with both.

29. Whoever violates provision of section 25 may, oil conviction be punished with fine which may extend to kyats 10,000.

30. Whoever abets or attempts or conspires in the commission of any offence under this Law shall be punished with the punishment provided for that offence in this Law,

CHAPTER XII: MISCELLANEOUS

31. The provisions of this Law shall not apply to State-owed Economic Organizations.

32. License holders have the right to form associations relating to their enterprise only by registering in accordance with the Myanmar Companies Act.

33. Offences prosecuted under this Law are prescribed as cognizable offences.

34. During the period in which the Government has not been able to form the Directorate under12, the duties and powers of the said Directorate shall be performed and exercised by the Directorate of Trade.

35. No suit or prosecution shall lie against any public servant for anything, which is done in good faith in pursuance of this Law.

36. For implementing the provisions of this Law, the Ministry concerned-

a. may with the approval of the Government, issue necessary procedures;
b. may issue necessary orders and directives.

RETAIL BUSINESS HOLIDAYS ACT, CANADA

Notice of Currency: This document is up to date.

This notice is usually current to within two business days of accessing this document. For more current amendment information, see the Table of Public Statutes – Legislative History Overview.

Amended by: 1991, c. 43, s. 1; 1993, c. 14; 1993, c. 27, Sched.; 1996, c. 34, ss. 1, 2; 1998, c. 18, Sched. G, s. 72; 2001, c. 9, Sched. D, s. 14; 2002, c. 17, Sched. F, Table.

Definitions

1. (1) In this Act,

"holiday" means,

(a) New Year's Day,
(b) Good Friday,
(c) Victoria Day,
(d) Canada Day,
(e) Labour Day,
(f) Thanksgiving Day,

(g) Christmas Day,

(h) Easter Sunday, and

(i) any other public holiday declared by proclamation of the Lieutenant Governor to be a holiday for the purposes of this Act; ("jour férié")

"municipality" means, except in section 7, a regional municipality and a local municipality, other than a local municipality within a regional municipality; ("municipalité")

"retail business" means the selling or offering for sale of goods or services by retail; ("commerce de détail")

"retail business establishment" means the premises where a retail business is carried on. ("établissement de commerce de détail") R.S.O. 1990, c. R.30, s. 1 (1); 1993, c. 14, s. 1; 1993, c. 27, Sched.; 1996, c. 34, s. 1 (1); 2002, c. 17, Sched. F, Table.

Holidays designated for closing

(2) The Lieutenant Governor may by proclamation declare any day that is a public holiday other than a day named in clauses (a) to (h) of the definition of "holiday" in subsection (1) to be a holiday for the purposes of this Act. R.S.O. 1990, c. R.30, s. 1 (2); 1996, c. 34, s. 1 (2).

Prohibition

2. (1) No person carrying on a retail business in a retail business establishment shall,

(a) sell or offer for sale any goods or services therein by retail; or

(b) admit members of the public thereto,

on a holiday.

Onus on employees, etc.

(2) No person employed by or acting on behalf of a person carrying on a retail business in a retail business establishment shall,

(a) sell or offer for sale any goods or services therein by retail; or

(b) admit members of the public thereto,

on a holiday. R.S.O. 1990, c. R.30, s. 2.

Exemptions: small stores

3. (1) Section 2 does not apply in respect of the carrying on of a retail business on a holiday where, on that day,

(a) the only goods available for sale by retail in the retail business establishment are,

(i) foodstuffs,

(ii) tobacco or articles required for the use of tobacco,

(iii) antiques, or

(iv) handicrafts,

or any combination of them, or where the principal business is the sale of goods referred to in subclauses (i) to (iv), or any of them, by retail and no other goods are available for sale except as sundries; and

(b) the number of persons engaged in the service of the public in the establishment does not at any time exceed three; and

(c) the total area used for serving the public or for selling or displaying to the public in the establishment is less than 2,400 square feet. R.S.O. 1990, c. R.30, s. 3 (1).

Idem, pharmacies

(2) Section 2 does not apply in respect of the carrying on of a retail business on a holiday in a pharmacy accredited under

the *Drug and Pharmacies Regulation Act*, where, on that day,

(a) the dispensing of drugs upon prescription is available to the public during business hours; and

(b) the principal business of the pharmacy is the sale of goods of a pharmaceutical or therapeutic nature or for hygienic or cosmetic purposes and no other goods are available for sale except as sundries; and

(c) the total area used for serving the public or for selling or displaying to the public in the establishment is less than 7,500 square feet. R.S.O. 1990, c. R.30, s. 3 (2); 1998, c. 18, Sched. G, s. 72.

Idem, special services

(3) Section 2 does not apply in respect of the carrying on of a retail business in a retail business establishment on a holiday where, on that day, the only goods available for sale by retail in the establishment are,

(a) gasoline and motor oil and, in conjunction therewith, other goods for consumption in the operation of a motor vehicle; or

(b) nursery stock or flowers, and in conjunction therewith, accessory gardening supplies; or

(c) fresh fruit or vegetables in respect of holidays falling between the 1st day of April and the 30th day of November of the same year; or

(d) books, newspapers or periodicals provided that no other goods are available for sale except as sundries, the number of persons engaged in the service of the public in the establishment does not at any time exceed three and the total area used for serving the public or for selling or displaying to the public in the establishment is less than 2,400 square feet.

Idem, art galleries

(4) Section 2 does not apply in respect of the carrying on of the retail business of an art gallery on a holiday, where on that day the number of persons engaged in the service of the public in the art gallery does not at any time exceed three and the total area used for serving the public or for selling or displaying to the public in the art gallery is less than 2,400 square feet.

Exemptions, under licences or other Acts

(5) Section 2 does not apply in respect of the sale or offering for sale by retail,

(a) of liquor under the authority of a licence or permit issued under the *Liquor Licence Act*;

(b) of goods or services under the authority of a tourist establishment licence issued under the *Tourism Act*.

Idem, education, recreation, amusement

(6) Section 2 does not apply in respect of the admission of the public to premises for educational, recreational or amusement purposes or in respect of the sale or offering for sale of goods or services incidental thereto.

Idem, necessary services

(7) Section 2 does not apply in respect of services sold in connection with the sale or offering for sale by retail of any goods permitted by this Act to be sold, and does not apply in respect of goods or services sold or offered for sale by retail in the form of or in connection with,

(a) prepared meals;

(b) living accommodation;

(c) laundromats and other coin-operated services;

(d) rentals of vehicles or boats;

(e) servicing and repair of vehicles or boats. R.S.O. 1990, c. R.30, s. 3 (3-7).

Tourism exemption

4. (1) Despite section 2, the council of a municipality may by by-law permit retail business establishments in the municipality to be open on holidays for the maintenance or development of tourism. 1991, c. 43, s. 1 (1).

Common pause day principle

(2) The council in passing a by-law under subsection (1) shall take into account the principle that holidays should be maintained as common pause days. 1991, c. 43, s. 1 (1).

Tourism criteria

(3) A by-law may be passed under subsection (1) only if there is compliance with the tourism criteria set out in the regulations made under this section. 1991, c. 43, s. 1 (1).

Application for by-law

(4) Subject to the regulations made under this section, the council shall consider a by-law under subsection (1) only on the application of one or more persons carrying on retail business in the municipality or on the application of an association, whether or not incorporated, representing persons carrying on retail business in the municipality. 1991, c. 43, s. 1 (1).

Local municipality

(5) In a regional municipality, the council of a local municipality may also apply for a by-law under subsection (1). 2002, c. 17, Sched. F, Table.

Public meeting

(6) Before passing a by-law under subsection (1), the council,

(a) shall hold a public meeting in respect of the proposed by-law;

(b) shall publish notice of the public meeting in a newspaper having general circulation in the municipality at least thirty days before the meeting is to be held; and

(c) shall permit any person who attends the public meeting the opportunity to make representations in respect of the proposed by-law. 1991, c. 43, s. 1 (1).

Council not obligated

(7) The council is not required to pass the by-law even if the tourism criteria are met. 1991, c. 43, s. 1 (1).

Commencement of by-law

(8) Subject to section 4.3, a by-law under this section comes into force on the thirty-first day after it is passed by the council. 1991, c. 43, s. 1 (1).

Procedures

(9) Subject to the regulations made under this section, the council may,

(a) establish procedures and fees for the processing of applications;

(b) combine two or more applications;

(c) hold one public meeting with respect to two or more applications;

(d) limit the number of applications that will be considered in any year. 1991, c. 43, s. 1 (1).

Regulations

(10) The Lieutenant Governor in Council may make regulations,

(a) prescribing tourism criteria for the purposes of this section;

(b) governing the procedures and fees for processing applications, the combining of applications and public meetings and limitations on the number of public meetings held by a council;

(c) setting out the contents of the application;

(d) requiring that a by-law that applies to a retail business establishment within such class of retail business establishments as may be set out in the regulation may be considered only on the application of the person carrying on the business. 1991, c. 43, s. 1 (1).

Idem

(11) A regulation under clause (10) (a) or (d) may classify retail business establishments and may prescribe different tourism criteria for the different classes of retail business establishments. 1991, c. 43, s. 1 (1).

Unorganized territory

4.1 The Lieutenant Governor in Council may by regulation permit retail business establishments in territory without municipal organization to be open on holidays. 1991, c. 43, s. 1 (1).

Contents of by-laws and regulations

4.2 A by-law under section 4 or a regulation under section 4.1,

(a) may apply to one or more retail business establishments or to one or more classes of retail business establishments;

(b) may apply to all or any part or parts of the municipality in case of a by-law or to all or any part of a territory without municipal organization in the case of a regulation;

(c) may limit the opening of retail business establishments on holidays to specific times or to a certain number of hours;

(d) may permit the opening of retail business establishments on some holidays and not on others;

(e) may restrict the opening of retail business establishments on holidays to specific periods of the year;

(f) may classify retail business establishments. 1991, c. 43, s. 1 (1).

Appeal to O.M.B.

4.3 (1) Any person who objects to a by-law made by the council of a municipality under section 4 may appeal to the Ontario Municipal Board by filing a notice of appeal with the Board setting out the objection to the by-law and the reasons in support of the objection.

Time for appeal

(2) The notice of appeal must be filed with the Board not later than thirty days after the day the by-law is passed by the council.

Dismissal without hearing

(3) The Board may, if it is of the opinion that the objection to the by-law set out in the notice of appeal is insufficient, dismiss the appeal without holding a full hearing, but before doing so shall notify the appellant and afford the appellant an opportunity to make representations as to the merits of the appeal.

Powers of O.M.B.

(4) The Board may,

(a) dismiss the appeal;
(b) dismiss the appeal on the condition that the council amend the by-law in a manner specified by the Board; or
(c) quash the by-law.

Commencement of by-law

(5) If one or more appeals are taken under this section, the by-law shall not come into force until,

(a) the day all appeals have been dismissed under subsection (3) or clause (4) (a); or
(b) the day the by-law is amended in the manner specified by the Board under clause (4) (b).

Correction of errors

(6) The Board may, without a hearing, correct an error in an order or decision under this section if the error arises from an accidental slip or omission.

Ontario Municipal Board Act, ss. 43, 95

(7) Sections 43 and 95 of the *Ontario Municipal Board Act* do not apply to an appeal under this section.

Time for decision

(8) The Board shall use its best efforts to decide appeals under this section within the period of time prescribed under subsection (9).

Regulations

(9) The Lieutenant Governor in Council may make regulations prescribing a period of time for the purpose of subsection (8). 1991, c. 43, s. 1 (1).

4.4 Repealed: 1993, c. 14, s. 2.

Sunday exception

5. (1) Despite any other provision of this or any other Act or the by-laws or regulations under this or any other Act, a retail business may be carried on in a retail business establishment on a Sunday if the retail business establishment is always closed to the public throughout another day of the week by reason of the religion of the owner of the retail business.

Definition

(2) For the purpose of subsection (1),

"religion of the owner" means,

(a) in the case of a sole proprietorship, the religion of the sole proprietor,

(b) in the case of a partnership, the religion named in a written agreement between the partners which is the religion of one of the partners,

(c) in the case of a corporation, the religion named in the by-laws of the corporation.

Affiliated corporation

(3) The exception set out in subsection (1) does not apply to a corporation that is the affiliate of another corporation unless all the retail business establishments in Ontario of the corporation and its affiliates close on the same day.

Deemed affiliation

(4) For the purposes of this section,

(a) a corporation shall be deemed to be affiliated with another corporation if one of them is the subsidiary of the other or both are subsidiaries of the same corporation or each of them is controlled by the same person; and

(b) the affiliates of every corporation shall be deemed to be affiliated with all other corporations with which the corporation is affiliated.

Deemed control

(5) For the purposes of this section, a corporation shall be deemed to be controlled by a person if,

(a) securities of the corporation to which are attached more than 50 per cent of the votes that may be cast to elect directors of the corporation are held other than by way of security only by or for the benefit of that person; and

(b) the votes attached to those securities are sufficient, if exercised, to elect a majority of the directors of the corporation.

Deemed subsidiaries

(6) For the purposes of this section, a corporation shall be deemed to be a subsidiary of another corporation if,

(a) it is controlled by,

(i) that other,

(ii) that other and one or more corporations each of which is controlled by that other, or

(iii) two or more corporations each of which is controlled by that other; or

(b) it is a subsidiary within the meaning of clause (a) of a corporation that is that other's subsidiary. R.S.O. 1990, c. R.30, s. 5.

Commercial tenants

6. A provision in a lease or other agreement that has the effect of requiring a retail business establishment to remain open on a holiday or on a Sunday or on December 26 is of no

effect even if the lease or agreement was made before section 2 of the *Boxing Day Shopping Act, 1996* comes into force. 1996, c. 34, s. 2.

Invalidity of certain municipal by-laws

7. (1) Subject to subsection (2), a by-law of a municipality passed under any other Act is invalid to the extent that it requires the closing of a retail business establishment on a holiday. R.S.O. 1990, c. R.30, s. 7 (1).

Transitional

(2) The following transitional rules apply to the by-laws of municipalities that were in force under this or any other Act at the end of the 30th day of November, 1991 and that relate to the opening or closing of a retail business establishment on holidays:

1. By-laws in force on the 3rd day of June, 1991 continue in force until the 1st day of December, 1992 or until the by-law is repealed, whichever is first.
2. By-laws that come into force on or after the 4th day of June, 1991 are repealed on the 1st day of December, 1991. 1991, c. 43, s. 1 (3).

(3) Repealed: 2002, c. 17, Sched. F, Table.

Penalty

8. (1) Every person who contravenes section 2 or a regulation under section 4 is guilty of an offence and on conviction is liable to a fine of not more than the greater of,

(a) $50,000; or

(b) the gross sales in the retail business establishment on the holiday on which the contravention occurred.

Idem, municipal laws

(2) A by-law under subsection 4 (1) requiring a retail

business establishment to be closed on a holiday shall provide that any person who contravenes the by-law is guilty of an offence and on conviction is liable to a fine of not more than the greater of,

(a) $50,000; or
(b) the gross sales in the retail business establishment on the holiday on which the contravention occurred.

Idem, coercion or counselling

(3) Every person who coerces, requires or counsels another person to contravene section 2, a regulation under section 4 or a by-law under subsection 4 (1) is guilty of an offence and on conviction is liable to a fine of not more than the greater of,

(a) $50,000; or
(b) the gross sales in the retail business establishment on the holiday in respect of which the offence under this subsection occurred. R.S.O. 1990, c. R.30, s. 8 (1-3).

Minimum penalty

(3.1) The minimum fine for an offence under this Act, other than for a contravention of subsection 2 (2), is $500 for a first offence, $2,000 for a second offence and $5,000 for a third or subsequent offence. 1991, c. 43, s. 1 (4).

Gross sales to be considered in determining fines

(4) In determining the amount of the fine, the court shall take into consideration any evidence respecting the gross sales in the retail business establishment on the holiday on which the contravention occurred.

Advertisements admissible as evidence

(5) A sign or advertisement giving the hours of a retail business establishment is admissible as evidence that the retail business establishment was open during those hours.

Determination of total area of a retail business establishment

(6) For the purpose of enforcing this Act or a by-law or regulation under this Act, the total area of a retail business establishment used for serving the public or for selling or displaying to the public on a holiday shall be deemed to be the greater of,

(a) the total area actually used on a holiday for serving the public or for selling or displaying to the public; and

(b) the total area normally used for serving the public or for selling or displaying to the public on days other than a holiday. R.S.O. 1990, c. R.30, s. 8 (4-6).

Court orders

9. (1) Upon the application of counsel for the Attorney General or of a municipality to the Superior Court of Justice, the court may order that a retail business establishment close on a holiday to ensure compliance with this Act or a by-law or regulation under this Act. R.S.O. 1990, c. R.30, s. 9 (1); 2001, c. 9, Sched. D, s. 14.

Idem

(1.1) In addition to its powers under subsection (1), the Superior Court of Justice, on the application of any interested person, may order that a retail business establishment close on a holiday to ensure compliance with this Act or a by-law or regulation under this Act. 1991, c. 43, s. 1 (5); 2001, c. 9, Sched. D, s. 14.

Idem

(2) An order under subsection (1) or (1.1) is in addition to any penalty that may be imposed and may be made whether or not a proceeding is commenced under the *Provincial Offences Act* for a contravention of section 2 or of a by-law or regulation under this Act. 1991, c. 43, s. 1 (6).

Glossary

Attractor: A significant tourist attraction, which compels visitation. The primary "must sees" in an area. The top reasons a tourist would choose to visit this area.

Audit: Audit is a systematic, documented, periodic, and objective evaluation and verification of how well a particular entity (company, product, program, individual, destination, etc.) is doing compared with a set of standards.

Biodiversity: Biodiversity means the variety of live forms, i.e., the different plants, animals, and microorganisms, the genes they contain, and ecosystems they form.

Business Travel: Travel for commercial, governmental or educational purposes with leisure as a secondary motivation.

Community: Community is people living in one place, district, state, or country (NEAP, 2000).

Confidential Tariff: A schedule of wholesale rates distributed in confidence to travel wholesalers and travel agents.

Consolidator: A person or company which forms groups to travel on air charters or at group fares on scheduled flights to increase sales, earn override commissions or reduce the possibility of tour cancellations.

Consumer Show: A product showcase for the general public. Differs from a "Trade Show" as a trade show generally targets industry professionals. Consumer Shows target the consumer. Often there is a charge to get into the show.

Convention and Visitors Bureau: These organizations are local tourism marketing organizations specializing in developing conventions, meetings, conferences and visitations to a city, county or region.

Conversion: Getting "heads in beds" or otherwise closing the sale. Differs from "hospitality." Hospitality is being warm, friendly and helpful. Conversion is active selling.

Country of Residence: Consists of the country where she/he has lived for most of the past year (12 months), or for a shorter period if she/he intends to return within 12 months to live there.

Cultural tourism: Cultural tourism is travel for the purpose of learning about cultures or aspects of cultures.

Culture: Culture is the sum total of ways of living by a group of human beings that is transmitted from one generation to another (NEAP, 2000).

Day visitors: Visitors who arrive and leave the same day for leisure, recreation and holidays, visiting friends and relatives, & business and professional.

Degradation: Degradation is any decline in the quality of natural or cultural resources, or the viability of ecosystems that is caused directly or indirectly by humans (NEAP, 2000).

Destination Marketing Organization (DMO): A company or other entity involved in the business of increasing tourism to a destination or improving its public image.

Destination Marketing: Marketing a city, state, country, area or region to consumers and trade.

Destination: The end point of a trip. This can be a town, a resort, or a stand-along attraction. The place to which a traveler is going; or any city, area, region or country be marketed as a single entity to tourists.

DMC (Destination Management Company): A local company that handles arrangements for tours, meetings, transportation, etc. for groups originating elsewhere.

DMO (Destination Marketing Organization): A company or other entity involved in the business of increasing tourism to a destination or improving its public image(such as a convention and visitor bureau).

Eco-labeling: Eco-labeling describes a scheme in which a product or service may be awarded an ecological label on the basis of its "acceptable" level of environmental impact.

Eco-Management and Audit System (EMAS): EMAS is a voluntary European Union regulation that strengthens ISO 14001 in key areas including public access and third party verification.

Ecotourism certification: Ecotourism certification programs are ones that cover businesses, services, and products that describe themselves as involved in ecotourism.

Ecotourism: "Responsible travel to natural areas that conserves the environment and improves the welfare of local people," according to The International Ecotourism Society. Ecotourism is "responsible travel to natural areas that conserves the environment and improves the welfare of local people," according to The International Ecotourism Society.

Environmental management system (EMS): EMS is part of the overall management system that includes the organizational structure, responsibilities, practices, procedures, processes, and resources for determining and implementing the environmental policy.

Familiarization Trip: A complimentary or reduced-rate travel program for travel agents, airline or rail employees or other travel buyers, designed to acquaint participants with specific destinations or suppliers and to stimulate the sale of travel. Familiarization tours, also called fam tours, are sometimes offered to journalists as research trips for the purpose of cultivating media coverage of specific travel products.

Foreign Independent Travel or Foreign Individual Travel (FIT): An international pre-paid unescorted tour that includes several travel elements such as accommodations, rental cars and sightseeing. A FIT operator specialises in preparing FITs documents at the request of retail travel agents. FITs usually receive travel vouchers to present to on-site services as verification of pre-payment.

Fulfillment Piece: Promotional literature, video, or other material that is sent in response to an inquiry. Usually contains full trip planning information.

Gross lettings: This refers to all room lettings, i.e. both paid & complimentary listings are included

Group Tour and Group Leader: Group Tour: a travel agent type company which plans motor coach trips. Group Leader: A small, informal group, such as a church group, scout troop, or social group. Usually one person plans the activities for the group. Some travel shows target these planners such as GLAMER.

Hospitality: A general term used in travel & tourism describing the "hospitality industry"; Refers to the general greeting, welcoming, food service, etc

Hotel Package: A package offered by a hotel, sometimes consisting of no more than a room and breakfast; sometimes, especially at resort hotels, consisting of (ground) transportation, rooms, meals, sports facilities and other components.

Incentive Tour: A trip offered as a prize, usually by a company to stimulate employee sales or productivity.

Inquiry: A request for more information about an attraction or destination.

International Organization for Standardization (ISO): ISO is a world federation based in Geneva to develop voluntary standards designed to facilitate international manufacturing, trade, and communications.

Interpretation: Print materials, signage, narration, guided tours, and anything that "interprets" the site for the visitor. Interpretation helps the customer "interpret" the experience and explains why a particular product is valuable. Interpretation adds value and meaning to the experience. Common interpretation techniques used in ecotourism include commentary on guided tours, presentations and discussions, drama performance, musical performance, brochures, signs, displays, and audiovisual presentations (NEAP, 2000).

Itinerary: A travel schedule provided by a travel agent for his/her customer. A proposed or preliminary itinerary may be rather vague or specific. A final itinerary however provides all details (flight numbers, departure times, reservation confirmation numbers) and describes planned activities.

Jungle tourism: Jungle tours have become a major component of green tourism in tropical destinations. A jungle is a subclimax tropical forest consisting of a tangled growth of lianas, trees and scrub which may form an almost impenetrable barrier to the tourist. Jungle tours are a relatively recent phenomenon of Western international tourism.

Key-informant survey: This involves interviewing people who are likely to have some insight into a problem: operating managers; sales staff; managers; suppliers; and consultants.

Keying: A social convention by which social 'reality' is transformed and seen as something else, such as the presentation of a fight as mere horseplay. In tourism, a peculiar, inverted variety of keying is frequently employed: the 'as if' situation in which participants are induced to playfully make believe that presented settings, activities or events are 'real', when as tourists they may be well aware that such occurences are contrived.

Leisure tourist: Leisure tourists, in contrast with business travellers, travel for pleasure and thus are not under any obligations to frequent specific destinations or facilities. They tend to be price and fashion conscious, concentrate their touristic activities to specific (vacation) times, and are influenced by marketing and publicity. Leisure tourism is heavily influenced by living standards, discretionary income levels and vacation entitlements.

Length of stay: This refers to the period of time which people spend in a destination. Many definitions require that visitors to a destination stay at least 24 hours or overnight, and less than one year, to be considered a tourist. Destination areas often look for means to extend tourists' length of stay in order to increase positive economic impacts.

Life Cycle assessment: Life Cycle assessment is a variant of an EMS that tracks a product, process or activity from "cradle to grave." In the tourism industry, it assesses the use of resources and social and environmental impact during three phases: 1) departure and return travel, 2) stay at the destination, and 3) activities at the destination.

Occupancy rate: A tourism business occupancy rate refers to the number of airline seats or the units of hotel room space sold. This demand is usually measured as a percentage of available seats or space occupied for a given period of time. It is calculated by dividing the number of occupied rooms/seats by the total number available for sale during the same period.

Outbound: Outbound tourism is defined as tourism involving residents of a country travelling to another country. Outbound tour operators offer package tours abroad. They either operate the tours themselves, or they commission the services of an inbound operator to handle local arrangements at the destination. The country from which the tourists originate is known as the generating market or country.

Package Tour: A saleable travel product offering an inclusive price with several travel elements that would otherwise be purchased separately. Usually has a predetermined price, length of time and features but can also offer options for separate purchase.

Packager: Anyone organizing a tour including prepaid transportation and travel services, usually to more than one destination.

Paid lettings: This refers to room lettings that are paid for by hotel guests

Product Extension: An add-on product or service, which enhances the experience of your product and generates additional revenue. Example: A state park that offers guided wildflower tours (for a fee).

Product Life Cycle: The cyclical pattern of demand for most products from "new and exciting" to "old and dated." Almost all products (tourism and otherwise) have these cycles.

Quality: In tourism, the product is often intangible and quality is not apparent until after it is consumed. Quality has been defined as zero defects or defections, but still may be defined by the customer. The International Organisation for Standardisation defines quality as 'the totality of features and characteristics of a product or service that bear on its ability to satisfy stated or implied needs'. Others believe that quality is a combination of outcome and processes, including internal and external conditions, and is obtained when the expectations and needs of customers are met.

Rack Card: The typical tourism brochure sized 4" x 9" and used primarily in tourism racks. Also known as a "teaser."

Rack Rate: The official cost posted by a hotel, attraction or rental car, but not used by tour operators.

Reassurance Sign: When trying to locate an attraction, especially when the route is long and unclear, it is critical to offer "reassurance signs" that tell the visitor they are indeed going the right way.

Receptive Operator: Someone who plans to "receive" your motorcoach or tour group. They may plan your lodging, meals, attraction visits, etc. for a fee or commission. A tour operator or travel agent specializing in services for incoming visitors, such as meeting them at the airport and facilitating their transfer to lodging facilities

Reconnaissance: An on-site evaluation of an attraction or destination from the perspective of the customer. Best performed by an outsider who is not familiar with the location and who is trained in fair and scientific methods of evaluation.

Resident: A person living in a given country, whether he is a national or not.

Retail Agency: Travel Company selling directly to the public, sometimes a subdivision of a wholesale and/or retail travel organization.

Southeast Tourism Society (STS): Established in 1983, STS has become the premier regional membership organization that promotes add develops tourism by pioneering programs that have a major impact on the tourism industry regionally and nationally. STS includes an eleven state region with 520+,members from every category of the tourism industry including in our sustaining member states.

Stakeholders: Stakeholders are, in the context of this report, environmentalists, park managers, tourism industry representatives, consumers, host countries, host communities, funders and financiers, and others who have an interest in a particular certification program.

Step-on Guide: A highly knowledgeable guide whom "steps-on" an incoming motorcoach and provides narrative interpretation for the experience. Some CVBs offer step-on guides for free. Sometimes an independent company offers this service for a fee.

Supplier: The actual producer of a unit of travel merchandise, such as a carrier, hotel or sightseeing operator.

Sustainable development: Sustainable development is that which "meets the needs of the present without Compromising the ability of future generations to meet their own needs."

Sustainable tourism: Sustainable tourism is, according to the World Tourism Organization, "envisaged as leading to management of all resources in such a way that economic, social and aesthetic needs can be fulfilled with maintaining cultural integrity, essential ecological processes, biological diversity, and life support systems." This is, according to the World Tourism Organisation, "envisaged as leading to management of all resources in such a way that economic, social and aesthetic needs can be fulfilled with maintaining cultural integrity, essential ecological processes, biological diversity, and life support systems."

Teaser Piece: A teaser piece can either be a rack brochure, or a mailer, giveaway, or some other promotional piece that is intended to "tease" the receiver into taking a specific action.

Tour Operator: A company that creates and/or markets inclusive tours and/or performs tour services.

Tour: Any prearranged (but not necessarily prepaid) journey to one or more places and back to the point of origin.

Tourism certification programs: Such as AAA (Automobile Association of America), have typically measured and compared quantity, service, and price, areas deemed most important to travelers.

Tourism Industries, US Department of Commerce: The federal agency responsible for tracking and analyzing international visitation to the United States.

Tourism Receipts: Tourism Receipts (TR) measures the total revenue received by Singapore from tourism activity. It includes all payments and prepayments for goods and services made by visitors, transit passengers, air & sea crew and foreign students (staying for one year or less) during their stay in Singapore. Visitors' payments to our national carriers (SIA & Silk Air) for international transport are also included.

Tourism: The business of providing and marketing services and facilities for pleasure travellers. Thus, the concept or tourism is of direct concern to governments, carriers, and the lodging, restaurant and entertainment industries and of indirect concern to virtually every industry and business in the world. Travel undertaken for pleasure. The business of providing and marketing services and facilities for pleasure travelers. Thus, the concept of tourism is of direct concern to governments, carriers, and the lodging, restaurant and entertainment industries and of indirect concern to virtually every industry and business in the world.

Tourist: Temporary visitor staying at least twenty-four hours in the country visited for a purpose classified as either holiday (recreation, leisure, sport and visit to family, friends or relatives), business, official mission, convention, or health reasons.

Travel Agent: The individual who sells travel services, issues tickets and provides other travel services to the travel services to the traveller sat the retail level.

Travel Industry Association of America: Travel Industry Association of America (TIA) is the non-profit umbrella trade organization of companies and government agencies representing all segments of the travel industry formed to promote travel to and within the US.

Underdevelopment: Within development theory, the concept of underdevelopment suggests that wealthy capitalist countries have held back the development of so-called Third World countries. Tourism in Third World destinations is controlled for the economic benefit of foreign owners, reinforces dependency, lacks involvement of local decision makers, leads to negative sociocultural impacts, and results in the promotion of staged attractions to capture an international tourism market.

Urban recreation: The concept of urban recreation covers recreational activity that takes place in an urban environment in contrast to a rural setting. Participants in such activities are either urban residents themselves, day visitors from rural areas, or tourists. The major activities are shopping, visits to heritage sites, museums, movie theatres, operas, sport and music events, and indoor sports activities.

Visitor Arrivals: Includes all who go through immigration clearance regardless of length of stay. This excludes the following: a.All Malaysian citizens arriving by landb.Returning Singapore citizens residing abroad c.Non-resident air and sea crew (except for sea crew flying in to join ship).

Visitor: Any person visiting a country other than that in which he has his usual place of residence for any reason other than following an occupation remunerated from within the country visited.

Visitors Centre: Travel information centre located at a destination to make it easier for visitors to plan their stay; often operated by a convention and visitors bureau, chamber of commerce or tourism promotion organisation.

Wholesaler: A company that purchases large blocks of rooms, tickets, etc. and then resells to either the public or to other travel professionals. A company that usually creates and markets inclusive tours and FITS for sale through travel agents. Usually sells nothing at retail (as opposed to a travel agent who can sell any product)., but also does not always create his/her own product; also less likely to perform local services

World Tourism Organisation: The World Tourism Organisation, a UN-related institution based in Madrid that collects data on tourism and lobbies on behalf of the industry.

World Travel and Tourism Council: The World Travel and Tourism Council (WTTC) is made up of chief executives from all sectors of the tourism industry, including accommodation, catering, cruises, entertainment, recreation, transportation and travel-related services. Its central goal is to work with governments to realise the full economic impact of tourism. Its millennium vision is to make tourism a strategic economic and employment priority, to move towards open and competitive markets, to pursue sustainable development, and to eliminate barriers to growth.

Yield percentage: To demonstrate the variable effect of both average price rates and occupancy rates, tourism managers develop a comparison focusing upon the yield rates during a given period of time. Managers can increase the yield rate (see yield management) by raising rates when demand is high.

Bibliography

Ashley, C, Boyd C and Goodwin, H (2000) 'Pro-P00r Tourism: Putting Poverty At The Heart Of The Tourism Agenda, Natural Resource Perspectives, Overseas Development Institute, London.

Bourke, Lisa, A. E. Luloff. 1995. "Leaders' Perspectives on Rural Tourism: Case Studies in Pennsylvania," *Journal of the Community Development Society*, Vol. 26, No. 2.

Bowling, M. 1992. "Illinois Rural Tourism: Do Rural Areas Benefit from Increases in Travel Expenditures," *Small Town*, Vol. 22, No. 4.

Dahms, Fredric. 1991. "Economic Revitalization in St. Jacobs, Ontario: Ingredients for Transforming a Dying Village into a Thriving Small Town," *Small Town*, Vol. 21, No. 6.

Edwards, J. Arwell, and Joan Carles Llures i Coit. 1996. "Mines and Quarries: Industrial Heritage Tourism," *Annals of Tourism Research*, Vol. 23, No. 2: pp. 341- 343.

Greater Johannesburg Metropolitan Council (GJMC), 2001: *Johannesburg 2030*, Corporate Planning Unit, GJMC.

Greater Johannesburg Metropolitan Council, 2002: Tourism Strategy, available at www.joburg/org.za

Green, Joslyn, Cheryl Hargrove, and Amy Jordan Webb. 1999. *Getting Started: How to Succeed in Heritage Tourism*. Washington, DC: National Trust for Historic Preservation.

Guglielmino, J. E. 1998. "Touring to Economic Health," *American Forests*, Vol. 103, No. 4: p. 31.

Kalish, A (2001) 'Tourism as Fair Trade: NGO Perspectives' Tourism Concern, London.

Kearsley G.W. (1997) Perceptions of Social and Physical Impacts upon New Zealand's Back Country Environments, in Opperman M. (ed) Pacific Rim Tourism, CABI Wallingford, 156-166.

Kearsley G.W. (1997). Wilderness Tourism: A New Rush to Destruction? Inaugural Professor Lecture. Centre for Tourism, University of Otago, Dunedin, New Zealand.

Kearsley G.W. and Higham J.E.S. (1996) Wilderness and Back Country Motivations and Satisfaction in New Zealand's Natural Areas and Conservation Estate, Australian Leisure (forthcoming).

Marcouiller, David W. 1997. "Toward Integrative Tourism Planning in Rural America," *Journal of Planning Literature*, Vol. 11, No. 3: pp. 337-357.

Mark A F (1990) Ecological and Nature Conservation Values: the case for a Conservation Park, in Kearsley G W and Fitzharris B B (eds) Southern Landscapes: Essays in honour of Ray Hargreaves and Bill Brockie, Department of Geography, University of Otago, Dunedin, 233-274.

Mastran, Shelley. 1997. *Getting Started in Heritage Area Development*. Washington, DC: National Trust for Historic Preservation.

Matovu, G., 2002: Policy options for good governance and local economic development in Eastern and Southern Africa, *Urban Forum*, 13, in press.

Maxwell, D., 2002: The importance of urban agriculture in food and nutrition, Available at www.ruaf.org

Mechling, Anne, and Paul Mechling. 1990. *Bed and Breakfast*. Proceedings of a Conference, April 9-12, 1989, Wheeling, West Virginia, pp. 328-330. Morgantown, West Virginia: West Virginia University Extension Service.

Middleton, Victor T. C., and Rebecca Hawkins. 1998. *Sustainable Tourism: A Marketing Perspective*. Woburn, Massachusetts: Butterworth-Heinemann.

Mieczkowski, Zbigniew. 1995. *Environmental Issues of Tourism and Recreation*. Lanham, Maryland: University Press of America.

Nielson J.M. and Endo R. (1977) Where have all the purists gone? An empirical examination of the displacement hypothesis. Western Sociological Review 8 (1), 61-75

Oelschlager M. (1991) The Idea of Wilderness : From prehistory to the age of ecology Yale University Press, New Haven and London.

Peberdy S. and Rogerson, C.M., 2000: Transnationalism and non-South African entrepreneurs in South Africa's small, medium and micro-enterprise (SMME) economy, *Canadian Journal of African Studies* 34, 20-40.

Roe, D, Leader-Williams, N and Dalal-Clayton (1997) 'Take only photographs, Leave only footprints: The environmental impacts of wildlife tourism' The International Institute for Environment and Development, London.

Roe, D. and Urquhart, P., 2001: *Pro-Poor Tourism: Harnessing the World's Largest Industry for the World's Poor*, International Institute for Environment and Development, London.

Schneider, Sandy S. 1993. "Advantages and Disadvantages of Tourism to an Agricultural Community," *Economic Development Review*, Vol. 11, No. 4: pp. 76-78.

Scott, G. and Pawson, E., 1999: Local development initiatives and unemployment in New Zealand, *Tijdschrift voor Economische en Sociale Geografie*, 90, 184-195.

Sem, John H. 1992. Tourism. *Proceedings of a Regional Conference*, October 16-18, 1991, Jackson, Mississippi. Southern Rural Development Center, Mississippi State University.

Sem, John, Mike Teskey, and Liz Watchorn. 1997. *Experiences and Benefits: A Heritage Tourism Development Model.* Ogden, Utah : U.S. Department of Agriculture, Forest Service.

Shah, K and Gupta, G (2000) 'Tourism, the Poor and Other Stakeholders: Experience in Asia', Overseas Development Institute (ODI) -Fair Trade in Tourism Paper, The Sustainable Livelihoods Working Paper Series, ODI, London.

Sharpley, Richard, and Julia Sharpley. 1997. *Rural Tourism: An Introduction*. London: International Thomson Business Press.

Shelby B., Vaske J.J. and Heberlein T. (1989) Comparitive analysis of crowding in multiple locations: results from fifteen years of research. Leisure Sciences 11 (4) 269-261

Shields, Peggy O., and Timothy J. Schibik. 1995. "Regional Tourism Marketing: An Analogical Approach to Organizational Framework Development," *Journal of Travel and Tourism Marketing*, Vol. 4, No. 1: pp. 105-113.

Smit, J. and Nasr, J. 1992: Urban agriculture for sustainable cities: using wastes and idle land and water bodies as resources, *Environment and Urbanization* 4 (2), 141-152.

Snow, Elinor R. 1994. *Farm Holidays and Ranch Vacations*. Beltsville, Maryland: Rural Information Center, National Agricultural Library, U.S. Department of Agriculture. Rural Information Center Publication Series No. 39.

South Africa, Republic of 1998: *The White Paper on Local Government*, Ministry for Provincial Affairs and Constitutional Development, Pretoria.

South Africa, Republic of, 2002: *Refocusing Development on the Poor*, Department of Provincial and Local Government, Pretoria (Confidential).

South Island High Country Review Working Party (1994) South Island High Country Review: Final Report, Ministers of Conservation, Agriculture and Environment, Wellington.

Squire, Shelagh J. 1996. "Literary Tourism and Sustainable Tourism: Promoting 'Anne of Green Gables' in Prince Edward Island." *Journal of Sustainable Tourism*, Vol. 4, No. 3: pp. 119-134.

Stabler, Michael J., ed. 1997. *Tourism and Sustainability: Principles to Practice*. New York: CAB International.

Stankey G.H. and Schreyer R. (1987). Attitudes towards wilderness and factors affecting visitor behaviour : A state of knowledge review Proceedings, National Wilderness Research Conference: Issues, state of knowledge and future directions. General technical Report INT-220. Intermontane Research station, Ogden UT. 246-293.

Stankey, G.H. 1973. Visitor perceptions of wilderness recreation carrying capacity. USDA Forest Service Research Paper. INT-142. Ogden, Utah 84401.

Theophile, Karin. 1995. "The Forest as a Business: Is Ecotourism the Answer?" *Journal of Forestry*, Vol . 93, No. 3: pp.: 25-27.

Thorgren, C., 1998: *Urban Agriculture in South Africa - The Perspective of Planners and NGOs in Cape Town*, Minor Field Studies No. 29, Swedish University of Agricultural Sciences, Uppsala.

UNDP (United Nations Development Programme), 1996: *Urban Agriculture: Food, Jobs and Sustainable Cities*, UNDP, New York.

Van der Berg, L., 2000: Urban agriculture as the combination of two 'impossible' though sustainable trends, Unpublished paper prepared for the Conference of the International Geographical Union Commission on Sustainable Rural Systems, Pusan, Korea, 8-13 August.

Vanderschueren, F., Wegelin, E. and Wekwete, K., 1996: *Policy Programme Options for Urban Poverty Alleviation: A Framework for Action at the Municipal Level*, Urban Management Programme Policy Paper No. 20, The World Bank, Washington DC.

Wall, G. 1997. "Is Ecotourism Sustainable?" *Environmental Management*, Vol. 21, No. 4: pp. 483-491.

Western Entrepreneurial Network. 1995. *Multi-Cultural Tourism Development Workbook*. Denver: University of Colorado at Denver, Colorado Center for Community Development.

Whitlock, Wendy, Kevin Van Romer, and Robert H. Becker. 1991. *Nature-Based Tourism: An Annotated Bibliography*. Clemson, South Carolina: Strom Thurmond Institute of Government and Public Affairs, Clemson University.

Index

O

P

Q

R

S

T